# MAU
# RIT
# IUS

**Travel with Marco Polo Insider Tips**

T0103373

# MARCO POLO TOP HIGHLIGHTS

## "BLUE MAURITIUS" ⭐1

Light as a feather and yet worth millions – the stamp that once decorated an invitation to a masked ball can today be admired in the Blue Penny Museum.

➤ p. 58, Port Louis

## CHAMP DE MARS ⭐2

Even those who never gamble should place a bet when the horse racing gets under way at the oldest course in the southern hemisphere.

📷 *Tip: For the best view, climb to the top of the Montagne de Signeaux.*

➤ p. 59, Port Louis

## CENTRAL MARKET ⭐3

Packed to the brim and a real treasure trove. Even upper-class ladies leave their remote mountain villages to shop here.

📷 *Tip: Get your camera flash ready and head to the souvenir and cloth merchants' area.*

➤ p. 62, Port Louis

## CAUDAN WATERFRONT ⭐4

This lively shopping centre is perfect for browsing, strolling or just enjoying the harbour views.

📷 *Tip: Enjoy the colourful parasols strung up above the street leading to the Blue Penny Museum.*

➤ p. 64, p. 65, Port Louis

### EUREKA – LA MAISON CRÉOLE ⭐5

Almost nothing has changed since 1830 in this colonial villa near Moka – you could almost think the family have just popped out.

➤ p. 68, Port Louis

### KALAISSON TEMPLE ⭐

Bursting with colour, this Tamil holy place in Abercrombie is a beautiful spot for quiet prayer, contemplation and ceremony.

📷 *Tip: Snap a photo of the prayer room; it is even brighter than the view outside.*

➤ p. 69, Port Louis

### VALLÉE DE FERNEY ⭐

Deep in this valley, the primeval forest of Mauritius has been restored, giving a glimpse of how the island once looked: dense jungle, with many birds, bats, lizards and deer.

➤ p. 77, The East

### ÎLE AUX CERFS ⭐8

Swim, snorkel, sunbathe. Despite the huge number of visitors, you can always find an idyllic spot on this beautiful beach.

📷 *Tip: Take an underwater camera to capture schools of fish – the noon sun will give you a wide, clear view.*

➤ p. 79, The East

### BLACK RIVER GORGES NATIONAL PARK ⭐

The island's largest hiking area, with 60km of trails through the rainforest (photo), is home to rare plants and birds like the Mauritian kestrel.

➤ p. 87, The Southwest

### CASELA NATURE PARKS ⭐10

A park full of adventure! Predator zoo, slides and a cable car over gorges. Or head out on safari on a quad bike, Segway or even a camel!

➤ p. 105, The West

# CONTENTS

THE NORTH

PORT LOUIS

THE WEST

THE EAST

THE SOUTHWEST

# CONTENTS

☉    Plan your visit          ☂ Rainy day activities

€-€€€ Price categories        🐖 Budget activities

(*)   Premium-rate            👪 Family activities
      phone number
                              ⚑ Classic experiences

                              🏝 Top beaches

(📖 A2) Refers to the removable pull-out map
(📖 a2) Additional map on the pull-out map
(0) Off the pull-out map

# BEST OF
# MAURITIUS

Icing-sugar sand at the foot of Morne Brabant mountain

# BEST ☂

## WHEN IT RAINS

**ACTIVITIES TO BRIGHTEN YOUR DAY**

### STROLL ALONG THE SEA BOTTOM

Don a helmet with air supply pumped in and a weight belt round your hips, you're good to go! This experience is offered by companies including *Solar Under Sea Walk* in Grand Baie. Don't forget an underwater camera!
➤ p. 49, The North

### A LEGENDARY POSTAGE STAMP

The Blue Mauritius postage stamp is a national treasure. For this reason it spends most of its day in darkness in the *Blue Penny Museum*. Make sure to ask beforehand about when they'll turn on the lights (photo).
➤ p. 58, Port Louis

### NATURE INSIDE

The *Natural History Museum* displays an amazingly realistic reconstruction of a dodo, along with more than 3,000 other exhibits covering the island's history, geology, and flora and fauna.
➤ p. 58, Port Louis

### PRECIOUS FABRICS

When it's grey outside, take refuge in this colourful dressmaker's paradise: the fabric stores lining *Corderie Street* in Port Louis.
➤ p. 66, Port Louis

### COOKIES FROM AN OLD RECIPE

In the Ville Noir district of Mahébourg, the Raults make cookies based on an old family recipe, using cassava roots. Visit the *Biscuiterie H. Rault* and try them for yourself – a real comfort when it's raining outside!
➤ p. 75, The East

### SHOP 'TIL YOU DROP

*Cascavelle Shopping Mall* outside Flic en Flac is an architectural delight. Open seven days a week, it offers everything you need to lift your spirits on a rainy day, from fashion, accessories and cosmetics boutiques, to cafés and snack bars.
➤ p. 106, The West

# BEST ON A BUDGET

## FOR SMALLER WALLETS

### SAY IT WITH FLOUR

The old *windmill* on the waterfront once ground flour for dock workers. Today, it houses a small museum illustrating how Mauritians lived 300 years ago. Free admission!

➤ p. 63, Port Louis

### AAPRAVASI GHAT

Take a free guided tour of *Aapravasi Ghat*, a former detention centre for immigrants arriving from India to find work on the sugar cane plantations. The site bears witness to colonial exploitation in the 19th century.

➤ p. 63, Port Louis

### A SYMPHONY IN THE PEDESTRIAN ZONE

Weekends come to life with instrumental music, singing and dancing around the harbour and pedestrian zone of the *Caudan Waterfront*, with local bands playing everything from pop and jazz to Mauritian sega and reggae. The atmosphere is incredible and the music is superb (photo).

➤ p. 65, Port Louis

### THE SHELL COLLECTOR

The poet *Robert Edward Hart* lived in a small house on the picturesque south coast in the mid-20th century. The façade is completely covered with mussels and coral, something that would be forbidden today. Inside, they've preserved the poet's furniture and personal belongings. Entry is free of charge.

➤ p. 92, The Southwest

### NATURAL WONDERLAND

Fresh grass, date palms, magnificent camphor trees, bananas and a small lake: Curepipe's *Botanical Garden* rivals its big brother in Pamplemousses but doesn't charge admission.

➤ p. 100, The West

# BEST WITH CHILDREN

## FUN FOR YOUNG & OLD

**SUNSET FUN**

Adults can enjoy the sunset with an exotic cocktail in hand, while the children run around and play in the swing chairs at *Veranda Pointe aux Biches*.

➤ p. 45, The North

**UNDERWATER TOURS**

*Blue Safari Submarine* allows guests insights into life under water. Its large windows will reveal fish, turtles and even shipwrecks! For children over 12, a ride on an underwater scooter is also a unique experience.

➤ p. 46, The North

**SLEEP IN A TENT**

The *Otentic Eco Tent* lodge in Deux Frères lets you stay close to nature: its "rooms" are tents on wooden platforms with integrated insect screens. The mattresses lie on wooden pallets,

and potato boxes serve as dressers. Solar panels provide electricity. A real adventure!

➤ p. 81, The East

**HOUSE OF ILLUSIONS**

The *Curious Corner of Chamarel* is incredible fun! This house of illusions and mysteries turns the world on its head. In one room you'll be walking on the ceiling of a kitchen; in another you'll look like a giant while others appear tiny.

➤ p. 86, The Southwest

**PREHISTORIC HIKE**

In the *Ebony Forest* in Chamarel, with its dense rainforest, wild animals, exotic plants and even an active volcano, you can discover what Mauritius looked like before humans arrived. Easy guided hiking trips are offered.

➤ p. 86, The Southwest

# BEST ⚑

## CLASSIC EXPERIENCES

**ONLY ON MAURITIUS**

### IT'S FISH-TASTIC AT THE HARBOUR

Most of Mauritius's harbours, like the one at *Grand Baie*, have fish landing stations, where fishermen sell the previous night's catch around noon. The colourful fish are just stunning!

➤ p. 47, The North

### SNACKS BY BIKE

Mauritians love snacks, and samosas, spring rolls and other options are sold everywhere – often from a bicycle! On the *beach at Grand Baie*, a veritable banquet can be purchased.

➤ p. 48, The North

### TRY ON A SARI

*Goodlands* is the shopping city of the north. It's always packed on market days, when farmers and traders bring their goods to town. Indian fashions are sold, as well as fruit, vegetables and spices. This is your best bet for a sari.

➤ p. 51, The North

### ON HORSEBACK

Horse racing has taken place on the *Champ de Mars* since 1812. Enjoy the carnival atmosphere at this traditional racecourse as all of Mauritius gathers to place their bets.

➤ p. 59, Port Louis

### CELEBRATE CHINESE NEW YEAR

The *Chinese New Year* here is all about the lucky colour red. The whole event comes to a close at the Caudan Waterfront, with tae kwon do performances, dragon dances and fireworks.

➤ p. 66, Port Louis

### DANCING ON THE HOT SAND

At weekends, Mauritian families meet at public beaches to picnic, arriving at spots like *Belle Mare* loaded with curries, rice, coffee and rum. The festive atmosphere grows until siesta time, when hammocks are stretched between the filaos trees (photo).

➤ p. 80, The East

# GET TO KNOW MAURITIUS

You'll struggle to sit still when people start dancing sega

# DISCOVER MAURITIUS

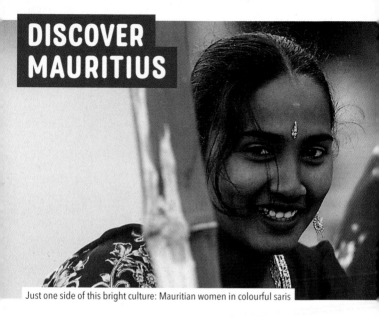

Just one side of this bright culture: Mauritian women in colourful saris

Mark Twain once said that God first created Mauritius, and then used it as the blueprint for paradise. There's certainly no shortage of evidence for that: white sandy beaches, turquoise bays, tropical forests and the warm smiles of the island's residents. Despite rising visitor numbers, this tropical paradise set in the Indian Ocean has lost none of its charm.

## INCREDIBLE DIVERSITY

Ready to rave all night and then crash out on the beach? Go for it! You can dance until dawn in Port Louis. Hoping for a spiritual kick? Visit a Hindu temple. Curious about the locals? Hop on a bus and head for the market. And if you spy a monkey on the way, hold out a banana and the once-shy creatures will let you get the photo of your trip!

**1511**
Portuguese seafarer Pedro Mascarenhas discovers the uninhabited island

**1598**
The Dutch land on Mauritius

**1710**
The Dutch leave and pirates settle on the island

**1715**
Mauritius is occupied by the French

**1748-1810**
The British repeatedly try to take the island

**1814**
Mauritius becomes a colony of the British Empire; the slave trade flourishes

## FROM LUXURY TO SIMPLICITY

Sure, there are plenty of five-star beach hotels where staff cater to your every whim. Not to mention wellness facilities to die for… But there are plenty of more affordable accommodation alternatives here too: rent a room with locals and learn to cook saffron chicken together, for example. In Mauritius, there's plenty of opportunity to choose between luxury and something more casual. There's choice when it comes to what you do, too, and sun worshippers will be just as happy here as fans of adventure sports. All kinds of people come to Mauritius, from globetrotters to film stars, and there's something for everyone on this island.

## THE LONG ROAD TO FREEDOM

In the 16th century, when Portuguese sailors discovered Mauritius, they found only a few species of birds, a tropical jungle, and a large lagoon. Next came the Dutch, who claimed part of the coast and named the island after their prince, Maurice of Nassau. They built houses and forts, planted sugar cane and imported red deer. The French settled here after the Dutch, and by the late 18th century, Port Louis was as important as Bombay or Calcutta. The island's strategic location made it a desirable stopover on the way to India. As such, the island was constantly fought over by the French and the British until the start of the 19th century, with the British capturing the colony in 1810. In March 1968, Mauritius finally became an independent, autonomous state and part of the Commonwealth.

**1835**
The abolition of slavery; workers are brought to the island from India and China

**1854-99**
Epidemics and natural disasters halve the population

**1968**
Mauritius becomes a sovereign state within the British Commonwealth

**1992**
Declaration of the Republic of Mauritius

**2015-2018**
Ameenah Gurib becomes the first woman President of the Republic

**2023**
Railway line opens from Rose Hill to Réduit via Ebène City

## A LONG HISTORY OF MULTICULTURALISM

As this island has no indigenous people, having once been uninhabited, every Mauritian is an "immigrant" of sorts. The population of today's Republic of Mauritius is composed of the descendants of Indians, French and Chinese people, and Arabs and enslaved people from Africa and Madagascar. From those many roots it developed a language, culture and music all of its own. You'll hear the rhythms of the African drum, European violin, Indian zither and Chinese lute here, while French *ragout*, Chinese noodles and Indian curry are all on the menu. Round the corner from the Catholic church you'll find the mosque, Hindu temple or Chinese pagoda. Because everyone was new here once, tolerance, solidarity and friendliness are a matter of the heart for the locals.

## EXTINGUISHED FIRE

The landscape of this tropical island is as diverse as its population. Mauritius was formed by volcanic eruptions in the sea around eight million years ago and, together with Réunion and Rodrigues, it belongs to the Mascarene Islands. Mauritius's volcano is now extinct, and the land is green and blossoming. The gradual sinking of the lava floor formed the coral reef that runs around almost the entire island and acts as a natural breakwater. This is what allows you to relax and swim in the warm, crystal-clear water. Even sharks are held at bay by the reef. Swimming, snorkelling, diving and boating are all popular here, thanks to the large amount of sunshine and pleasant air temperature of around 24–30°C. If you find yourself longing for a gentle breeze on a hot day between November and March, head for the east coast, where the trade winds blow. Alternatively, if you're after stillness and sunshine in the cooler months (May to August), try the sheltered west of the island. And while the coast is a big draw, it's worth remembering that 40 per cent of the island is pretty hilly! We're talking 300m above sea level, with forests and waterfalls. So don't forget your hiking boots.

## NOT ALL SUGAR AND SPICE

Most of the Mauritian population lives relatively modestly, with many locals working as small-scale entrepreneurs, trying to make a living by offering their services and renting out rooms in their houses to holidaymakers. For many decades, sugar was the main source of income on the island, until subsidies were removed and prices dropped on world markets. As you land, you'll still see miles and miles of sugar-cane fields, but out of 30 sugar factories, only four survive. The government stepped in with incentives that attracted other industries, mostly textile factories, to the country, while at the same time the tourist market was developed, with hotel complexes, villas and golf courses. However, Mauritius has so much more to offer than beach holidays; it is definitely worth heading into the interior on a discovery tour with a rental car. Keep your eyes and ears open as you travel around the island, and you'll soon discover its unique magic.

# AT A GLANCE

## 1.3 MILLION
**POPULATION**

Birmingham: 1.15 million

## 62 per cent
of Mauritians
are of Indian descent

## 160km
**of beaches**

A coral reef surrounds almost
the entire island, providing safe
swimming

## 1,865km$^2$
**area**

Mallorca is twice as big
London: 1,572km$^2$

**HIGHEST MOUNTAIN**

## 828m

**PITON DE LA PETITE
RIVIÈRE NOIRE**

Ben Nevis: 1,345m

**COLDEST MONTH**

## AUGUST
## 19°C
The seasons are reversed in the southern
hemisphere

## LOVE ISLAND

Mauritius is the world's most popular place for destination
weddings, with 12,000 couples coming here to marry every year

## DODO

The long-extinct bird still
symbolises the island

**MAURITIA**
The sunken continent
under Mauritius

**AVERAGE AGE: 30.8**
UK: 40.7

# UNDERSTAND MAURITIUS

**INSIDER TIP**
**Test your language skills**

*L'Edikasyon pu Travayer* has a school that offers language lessons to tourists *(tel. 2 08 21 32 | lalitmail@ intnet.mu).*

## THE MAURITIAN ROYAL ROAD

There is a *Route Royale* in nearly every town and village in Mauritius. It's generally the name of the main street, and often lined with shops and restaurants. Since there are no building or house numbers, it's best to ask a local for directions if you're looking for somewhere specific. Or simply drive slowly along the *Route Royale*, often called *Royal Street* or *Royal Road*, until you find the place you're looking for.

## BONJOUR, HELLO, BONZOUR

Locals will switch from French to English to Creole in a single sentence, without so much as a blink of the eye. The language of government is English, the upper classes speak French, and people use Creole among themselves in their everyday lives. Creole is similar to French, but peppered with Malagasy, Indian and English words.

Despite the fact it is most of the population's native language, Creole is rarely taught in schools. There are, at least, TV news bulletins in Creole, but newspapers are published in French. Hindu, Chinese and Arabic are all also spoken by minorities. In fact, there are a total of 22 languages spoken on the one island!

As a visitor, you can get by speaking French or English, but if you fancy chatting to the locals in Creole,

## FINDING MARLIN

A relatively short way beyond the coral reef, the sea around Mauritius becomes very deep, making it ideal for deep-sea anglers. The most commonly hunted fish in these waters is the blue marlin (swordfish), which can often weigh more than 300kg. November to April is the best time to head out to sea in search of these fish. You can find fishing gear and other equipment everywhere along the coast, but anglers should be aware that fishing by ships with trawl nets has depleted the stock, meaning you will need some patience!

## EXPENSIVE ERROR

When the nobility received their invitations to Governor Gomm's masked ball in 1847 – with the Blue Mauritius stamp stuck to the envelopes – no one could have guessed that people would one day queue up to see this tiny stamp!

Today, one blue two-penny stamp and one red one-penny stamp are proudly on display in the Blue Penny Museum in Port Louis. The tiny treasures are fiercely guarded – the spotlight in the dark basement room is switched on for just ten minutes every hour. That's as much as the tiny blue stamp, its value stretching into the millions, can tolerate without fading. Why are they so valuable? The stamps were actually the product of a misprint. The somewhat deaf and forgetful engraver, Joseph Barnard, engraved the words "Post Office" next

*St Géran* back to Mauritius, but the boat is wrecked on a reef off the island. The girl drowns in the waves in front of Paul, who's watching from the shore. He later dies of a broken heart.

Fancy a quick chat with the locals? Most Mauritians speak English

to a picture of Queen Victoria on a copperplate for these, the first Mauritian stamps. Shortly afterwards, it was realised that he should have used the inscription "Post Paid" instead. This meant new stamps had to be printed after the ball – but the mistake on the originals led them to become wildly sought-after collectors' items.

## PAUL & VIRGINIE

Paul, from a humble background, and Virginie, a wealthy girl, discover their love for each other. Virginie, however, is sent to France for her education. Longing for Paul, she embarks on the

With his novel *Paul et Virginie* (1788), French author Jacques-Henri Bernardin de Saint-Pierre created not only a monument to love, but also an indictment of class arrogance and slavery. Today you can follow the traces of Paul and Virginie all over the island – as if they had actually lived. Monuments have been dedicated to them in Port Louis and in Curepipe, and it's claimed that Virginie and her mother visited the church in Pamplemousses. Restaurants and hotels are named after them, and you can buy the book's illustrations in the form of pricy engravings or printed on T-shirts.

Villa Eureka has no need for air-conditioning because it has so many doors

There's also a monument in Poudre d'Or to the *St Géran*, a real ship that was actually wrecked on the north coast in 1744; parts of the wreck can be seen in the museum of Mahébourg.

## SIR SEEWOOSAGUR RAMGOOLAM

This name is long but encountered all over Mauritius. The airport, the Botanical Garden, the largest hospital and many other institutions carry the name. Ramgoolam was born in Mauritius in 1900, the son of Indian parents. After studying in Britain, he returned to his homeland and soon afterwards began fighting for the island's autonomy. From 1948, he was chairman of the Labour Party, which campaigned for Mauritian independence from Britain. This goal was achieved in 1968, and Ramgoolam

became the island's first prime minister. His tenure lasted until 1982. After his party lost its majority he held the office of governor general, a ceremonial position with few actual powers. Ramgoolam died in 1985. He's known in Mauritius as the "father of the nation" and the "architect of independence".

## COOL DRAUGHTS

Long before the electric fan, let alone air-conditioning, the inhabitants of the island's elegant colonial houses had to settle for cool draughts. The best example of building to maximise draughts can be found at *Villa Eureka* near Moka, with its 109 doors. Once they're all opened, the draught is really very pleasant. A covered veranda also runs round the building providing shade. To prevent the whole house from going up in flames in the event of a fire, the furniture was crafted from flame-retardant precious woods like mahogany. As a precaution, the kitchen was also housed in an annex built of stone.

Inside, you can wander over the creaking floorboards of the house's eight rooms. The table is still set with silver plate and crystal glasses, the grand piano is open, the curtains are billowing, just as if former owner Eugène Le Clézio was about to return at any moment. Today's owner, Jacques de Maroussem, has left everything as it was; the villa hasn't been changed architecturally since 1830.

### ECO FOOTPRINT

As soon as the first explorers landed, Mauritius began to lose its unique natural habitat: rainforests were cut down and animal species became instinct; fishermen set out with dynamite and harpoons, while ships anchored on the coral reef, damaging both reef and seabed.

Since then, countless initiatives have been launched to raise awareness of the environment. The NGO *Reef Conservation Mauritius* works to restore the coasts and reef. Their team members go into schools to teach children about ecology and recruit them for climate activities, such as mangrove planting. Similarly, conservationists from the *Mauritian Marine Conservation Society* take anchor buoys out to sea for boats to moor on, ensuring neither fish nor underwater plants are endangered.

## TRUE OR FALSE?

### I DO!

An underwater wedding really is the experience of a lifetime. Forget French or English, you need to brush up on your diving signs to communicate at the bottom of the ocean. So what's the sign for "You may kiss the bride"? And how do you kiss? It's not so easy in diving gear! Getting married under water is certainly an unusual choice, but 30 couples say "I do" every day on Mauritius – whether on a hotel beach, in a colonial-era house, on a sailing boat or, yes, even under water!

### ISLAND ROMANCE

Even Nobel Prize winners in literature like Jean-Marie Gustave Le Clézio aren't immune to romanticising the island. The main characters in *Alma* (2020), for example, hail from a family of wealthy plantation owners, the likes of which are rarely found in reality. Le Clézio paints a mythical picture of the island, whose lush landscapes have long since partly given way to hotels and shopping centres. A woman gives birth in the forest as a matter of principle, while a man invokes spirits. Yet the spirituality of the Creole population and their closeness to nature are as clichéd as the island's endless white-sand beaches.

## EVERYTHING MADE FROM SUGAR

Some 80 per cent of the island's agricultural land is cultivated with sugar cane, and it's said that the island of Mauritius has two landscapes: one before and one after the annual sugarcane harvest. Shafts of sugar cane come in wine-red, brown and green-white. Each holds around 20 litres of juice, from which about two kilos of sugar can be made. Sugar cane is harvested in July and December. The metre-high canes are taken to factories, ground in massive mills and boiled down to brown juice in boilers. Centrifuges are then used to separate granulated sugar from molasses.

The dodo was quite an odd bird

Visitors can witness the process for themselves in *L'Aventure du Sucre* (see p.42), a new, very informative sugar museum near Pamplemousses.

However, there is a flip side to the economic success of sugar: after decades of an economic boom thanks to preferential prices and purchase guarantees on the world market, a ruling by the World Trade Organization (WTO) put an end to the subsidies. Now, sugar producers are more involved in processing the by-products of the sugar refinery: molasses is used to distil rum, and bagasse (the fibrous material left after crushing sugar cane to extract its juice) is processed into bio fuels or used to make construction panels.

## THE DODO

Plump body, short little legs, stumps where there should be wings: this is the dodo. "It looked like a chicken, but was twice the size of a swan," noted Dutch explorer Admiral van Neck in his diary in 1598. The strange creature lived guilelessly on this island full of ebony forests, mahogany and teak trees, in thickets of lianas, ferns and orchids. It couldn't fly and hatched its eggs on the ground, both factors in its undoing as it became easy prey for settlers and sailors alike. It was hunted for fun and food.

One hundred years after van Neck wrote his description, the dodo was extinct. But its untimely demise only fuelled its legendary status: today, replicas are available on everything from bath towels to fridge magnets, and cuddly toy dodos abound. If you want to see the original, there is a reconstruction of a dodo skeleton on display in the Natural History Museum in Port Louis. That is the closest you'll get these days to the bird.

## STORMY TIMES

Here, cyclones are a force of nature almost everyone is afraid of. During this weather phenomenon, nobody is allowed out, the electricity fails, the freezer starts to defrost and any delicious treats frozen for the holidays are brought out to avoid wasting them. At least children get to enjoy the treats, the family time and games of dominoes that happen when a state of emergency is declared.

Cyclones are whirlwinds that occur between December and April. They form over the Indian Ocean near the equator when the water is warmer than 26°C for an extended period and evaporates very quickly. Statistically, a cyclone crosses the island every 20 years, reaching speeds of 250kmh. That said, the tails of storms hit three or four times a year, bringing strong winds and rain. Mauritius has a four-stage warning system to ensure no one is caught by surprise and that everyone can stock up on water, candles and tinned food, and lock their doors and windows in good time. People who live in sheet metal huts take shelter in public buildings.

## SEGA NIGHT FEVER

The one common language of Mauritius's slaves was music. After all, how else could labourers torn from their homes in Africa and India communicate? They played simple instruments like the triangle, the *maravane* (a box filled with grains), the *bobre* (a steel string stretched over a gourd) and the *ravanne* (a flat drum), and improvised and danced.

Until the 1980s, hardly anyone outside the Creole population took sega music seriously, even though it was an essential part of any local celebration. As time went on, however, hotels discovered its potential as tourist entertainment, even if in a rather watered-down form. For a more authentic experience, head to a concert by an artist such as Cassiya. The songs touch on love but also alcoholism and drugs. Sometimes sega integrates other influences like Indian pop music or reggae, when it makes – what else? – "seggae".

## FILAOS

You're not the only one sweating in the tropical heat; the filaos, also called *casaurinas*, are too. Sit underneath one and you will feel tiny beads of water dripping down on you. These delicate trees were introduced from Australia in the 18th century. Today's dense groves cover the vast majority of the coast. Filaos provide more shade than coconut palms and they like growing in the slightly salty ground of the beach. While strong, the tree's trunks and branches are flexible enough to bend and give way during severe hurricanes and cyclones. Their appearance recalls that of the European larch.

# EATING
# SHOPPING
# SPORT

If you're getting bored on the beach, why not set sail on a boat?

# EATING & DRINKING

There is an incredible variety of cuisine on the island, whether you choose to eat in a gourmet restaurant or at a roadside food stall. Just remember: if you're not staying in Grand Baie, Péreybère or Flic en Flac, you'd do well to book half-board accommodation because restaurants are difficult to reach from most holiday resort hotels.

## A WORLD OF TRADITION

Every group that settled on the island over the centuries, whether Chinese, African, Indian or French, brought their own culinary traditions and dishes with them. Over time, these merged into local dishes. A Mauritian Hindu will prepare *biryani* without beef, for instance, substituting lamb or chicken instead.

What you will soon notice is that Indian cuisine rather dominates, as does the scent of cumin, cardamom and coriander. Curries are refined with turmeric and occasionally also coconut milk, cloves, cinnamon or tamarind paste.

Generally speaking, people here enjoy their spice. That said, hotel cooks tend to avoid large amounts of chilli like the plague. Ask for a *rougaille* (tomato sauce with onions and chilli) to pile on the heat in just a few pinches if you like your food spicy. Outside the hotels, things can be different. There is an actual scale for spiciness: the Scoville scale. It ranges from zero (neutral) to ten (explosive) – *gâteaux piments* (Mauritian chilli cakes, see below) are rated an eight!

## CURRY FOR LIFE

Everyday foods here are *cari (curry)*, *daube* (a soup-like ragout) and *rougaille* – this richly flavoured, spicy sauce, seasoned with masala, turmeric and coriander, provides the base for

A world of flavour awaits: from curry (left) to samosas (right)

meat, poultry and fish dishes and is the icing on the cake of any main course. *Vindaye* is a dish made from pieces of meat or fish simmered in a sauce made of ginger, garlic and vinegar. Side dishes include rice, lentils and beans *(grains)*, or *brèdes* (steamed vegetable leaves) and *chatini*, a freshly prepared mixture of raw tomatoes and chilli. The Indian custom of adding flatbreads *(rotis, nans* or *faratas)* to a meal is popular across the island, but sometimes you'll also get a baguette.

## A QUESTIONABLE TREAT

On holidays and special occasions, locals like to treat themselves to an expensive delicacy: the nutty and tender palm heart salad *(coeur de palmiste)*. The soft heart of the trunk is grated and dressed with vinegar, oil and lemon juice. It's a rare delicacy because a palm tree has to be felled to make this salad.

## MIX TO THE MAX

Hotel buffets are a good opportunity to taste your way around the island, especially a "Paul & Virginie buffet", which includes typical Creole dishes. Starters might include smoked marlin, the aforementioned palm hearts and squid salad, while mains are tasty curries with chicken, fish or pork alongside vegetables such as white beans and aubergines. For vegetarians, Indian vegetable or tofu curries are the way to go. An absolute must-try are *gâteaux piment*. But enjoy with caution! These deep-fried balls are made of a thick, white bean paste, and spiced with hot chilli pieces. Buffet desserts usually comprise fruit salads and custard-type puddings.

INSIDER TIP
Hot stuff!

## A DIFFERENT KIND OF FINGER FOOD

The traditional plates here are banana leaves, and there's no need for cutlery when eating Mauritian-style. Instead, you use your thumb, index and middle fingers as a kind of "hand fork". Conventional cutlery should be available, too, but that is the way the Creole people like it. This way, the aroma unfolds more intensively, the scent enters the nostrils more quickly and you get full faster. Or at least that is what the Mauritians claim. The Creole take on finger food is usually served at picnics or at home, but not in restaurants.

## FROM RELAXED & CASUAL TO TRULY SNAZZY

You can expect everything on Mauritius, from simple Creole snacks to bistros and pizzerias, and French gourmet cuisine in five-star hotels. For the largest and most varied range of eateries, Port Louis is the place to be. Most restaurants are open for lunch from noon to 2pm and in the evening from 6pm; it's difficult to find anything still open after 9.30pm. In hotels, the kitchen usually stays open all day. A good tip is to always wait at the restaurant entrance for a waiter to escort you to your table.

## FOLLOW YOUR NOSE

The island's roads are full of Creole restaurants sitting next to Chinese, Indian, Japanese, Thai and European eateries. But if you're on an island tour, stop at one of the simple, affordable so-called "snacks" (snack bars) and try boiled or fried noodles (mine bouille or mine frite) or samosas (samoussas) filled with meat, fish or vegetables. These are either sold from stalls in front of bistros or simply from a stand attached to a bicycle. They only cost a few rupees, and – don't worry – there are hygiene regulations on the island.

## ALCOHOLIC DRINKS

Several varieties of beer are brewed at the local Phoenix brewery: Phoenix, Blue Marlin and Stella Pils are the most popular, and all stand up to international comparisons. Wine is also popular. The South African and French wine sold on Mauritius is very good, and there's usually a large selection in the supermarkets and corner shops, and of course on restaurants' and bars' drinks menus. Rum, of varying qualities, is available everywhere. The cocktails and rum-based mixed drinks (punches) are absolutely delicious.

## NON-ALCOHOLIC

What would a tropical island be without fresh fruit cocktails? Somehow they taste best at the market, made from freshly squeezed mango and pineapple juices, and coconut milk. You should definitely try an aromatic lassi (a yoghurt drink) and coconut milk served in a coconut at least once during your visit. A drink made from lemongrass is a refreshing choice in the heat of the day: the leaves are boiled briefly in water and the brew is then cooled and sweetened with sugar syrup. Coffee addict? You'll find it in every hotel, but tea is generally the islanders' preferred drink.

## Today's specials

### Starters

**SAMOUSSAS**
Crispy triangular pastries fried in oil, with various savoury fillings

**GÂTEAUX PIMENTS**
Spicy, deep-fried dough balls made of chickpea flour, coriander and chilli

**SALADE D'OURITE**
Squid salad with thyme, cumin, coriander and chilli

### Mains

**CURRY DE POULET**
Chicken, tomatoes, onions and masala powder cooked together and served with rice and broad beans

**CURRY D'AGNEAU**
Mild lamb curry dish, flavoured with coconut sauce and raisins

**BIRYANI**
A spicy rice dish prepared with slices of meat, some eggs and vegetables

**ROUGAILLE DE BOEUF**
A kind of beef stew in a spicy tomato sauce

### Desserts

**GÂTEAU PATATE**
A cake made from sweet potatoes and vanilla

**PUDDING DE MANIOC**
Juicy manioc pudding

**VERMICELL**
Vermicelli with milk, grapes and cardamom

### Drinks

**ALOUDA**
Jelly-like milkshake made with agar-agar and basil seeds

**LASSI**
Indian yoghurt drink with mango or other fruit

**TI-PUNCH**
Aperitif, mix of rum, lime and sugar

**RHUM ARRANGÉ**
Digestif, rum mixed with vanilla and herbs

# SHOPPING

### FROM LUXURY TO RELAXED

The most popular shopping centres on the island include the *Orchard Centre* in Quatre Bornes, the *Trianon Shopping Centre* (off the motorway on the outskirts of Quatre Bornes) and the *Cascavelle Shopping Mall* on the road to Flic en Flac. The relaxed *Caudan Waterfront* in Port Louis even comes with a harbour view, while *La Croisette* in Grand Baie is the place for the elegant shopper. *Les Galleries Evershine* in Rose Hill is popular with Mauritians.

### FOR SMART SPENDERS

Head to the supermarket for reasonably priced spices, syrup and rum. Household goods shops are also a good choice and great for browsing. You can buy things cheaply at markets, where you will see fruit and vegetables sold next to clothes, fabrics, baskets, crockery and tourist tat. There are markets at *Abercrombie (Tue, Sat/Sun), Centre de Flacq (daily), Curepipe (Wed, Sat), Goodlands (Tue, Fri), Mahébourg (Mon), Port Louis (daily)* and *Quatre Bornes (Thu, Sun clothes market; Wed, Sat vegetable market only).*

### THE EMPEROR'S NEW CLOTHES

Head to *Karl Kaiser* in Arsenal for good-quality menswear. You can also have suits sailor-made here. The shopping malls, meanwhile, are the place to go for fabrics, t-shirts and towels. And while it may be hot outside, it's still worth taking a look at the fine cashmere and knitwear! If you are on the hunt for a bargain, try a factory outlet or the small shops in the Sunset Boulevard shopping complex in Grand Baie. Most five-star hotels also have special offers at the end of the season.

The island's markets offer all manner of objects to brighten up your everyday life at home

## SWEET TEMPTATION

Note the difference: *rhum agricole* is made from fresh sugar-cane juice, while *rhum industriel* is made from molasses, the by-product of sugar extraction. The former is more aromatic, and the most famous brands are *Green Island* and *Saint Aubin*. Pure rum or versions flavoured with vanilla or coffee beans are available. In the *Rhumerie Chamarel* you can buy white sugar-cane liquors and a type of alcohol that's distilled like cognac.

## FLOWERS TO GO

The red, heart-shaped anthurium is a popular souvenir. You can order them by phone at *Sun Souvenir (tel. 6 37 37 84)*. You'll receive your bouquet at the airport, packed and ready to fly.

## REAL SPARKLERS

Diamonds and other imported gems are cut and polished here. Some factories have showrooms selling jewellery for duty-free export. The most famous diamond workshops and jewellers are *Adamas* (p. 103), *Caunhye Bijoux* and *Goldfinger* (p. 66), which have branches in hotels and shopping centres. A visit to goldsmith *Bernd Wilhelm* (p. 99) is a dazzling experience.

## SMALL IS BEAUTIFUL

If you must have a dodo, why not choose one made of silver by extrovert jeweller *Patrick Mavros*? *(Beau Plan | tel. 2 60 43 33 | patrick mavros.com)*. He gave Kate, Princess of Wales, a brooch to mark the birth of Prince George. In fact, Kate is a self-confessed fan of his work, which is inspired by monkeys, crocodiles and elephants. Book in advance on the website or by phone.

**INSIDER TIP** Royal dodo!

# SPORT & ACTIVITIES

### CYCLING TOURS
The low-traffic stretches along the east coast are particularly suitable for cycling tours. Great routes can be found on the Blue Bay peninsula in the southeast, at Morne Brabant, and on the northern tip of the island at Cap Malheureux. Mountain bikers can find more demanding routes in the Black River Gorges National Park. Almost all hotels hire out bikes.

### DIVING
There are over 30 diving centres in Mauritius, all offering courses and equipment hire. For a challenge, you will want to head to the north of the island where you can go wreck diving on the *Silver Star*: free descent, swim around the ship, carefully glide inside and wave to the giant puffer fish in the bow!

Over in the west, venture through the reef crevice and into the 12m *Cathedrale* cave. The sunlight that reaches into the cave transforms the underwater world into a mystical blue empire.

For tips on other great diving spots in the region, get in touch with the diving professionals at *Abyss (tel. 57 22 49 90)* in Flic en Flac.

### EXTREME SPORTS
The *Royal Raid (royalraid.com)* race is held every May/June. Long-distance runners train in the canyons of the Black River and on the slopes of Le Pouce from November for courses covering 65km, 30km and 12km.

At *Vallée des Couleurs (tel. 6 60 44 77 | lvdc.mu/en/ zipline)* you zip along a 1.5km-long steel cable, the longest zipline in the Indian Ocean. Try to relax and enjoy the deer grazing below! An alternative adrenaline rush is the river

**INSIDER TIP** Need for speed?

A rather soggy adventure: a canyoning tour at the Tamarin waterfalls

trek at the *Eau Bleue* waterfall. *Motrek Adventures (tel. 59 13 55 12 | motrek adventures. wixsite.com/ trekking)* will take you down into the depths, well secured by a rope. *Vertical World (Curepipe | tel. 6 97 54 30 | vertical worldltd.com)* offers canyoning, and in Grand Baie you can float over the water on a flyboard with *Flyn' Dive (tel. 52 57 22 44 | flyndive.mu).*

## GOLF

You have plenty of choice here, ranging from five easy-to-play nine-hole courses for beginners to eight first-class 18-hole championship courses. Rather conveniently, most of the courses belong to hotels and guests can play without paying a green fee.

Two beautiful courses line the *Long Beach Golf & Spa Resort (long beachmauritius.com/en).* Just as great are the *Île aux Cerfs* golf course *(ile auxcerfsgolf.com)*, on an island off

Mauritius, and the *Anahita Golf Club* at the *Four Seasons Resort Mauritius (fourseasons.com/mauritius/golf)*, with views of mountains, forests and a lagoon. You can also tee off there as a non-hotel guest. The west coast has a public course, *Tamarina (Tamarin | tamarina.mu)*. Golfers can also become temporary members of the *Gymkhana Club* in Vacoas *(mgc.mu)*. The *Avalon* golf course *(Bois Sec | avalon.mu)* is situated at a lofty height near the tea plantations. Also open to the public is *Mont Choisy (mont choisygolf.com)* in the resort of the same name in the north.

## HIKING & MOUNTAINEERING

You'll need some muscle power to climb the 556m-high Le Morne Brabant, the island's most prominent mountain. The reward is the view! Tours head off to the *Montagne du Lion* (480m) at Vieux Grand Port and

_Le Pouce_ (812m) at Port Louis, both with beautiful views from their summits. And climbing fans can scale _Pieter Both_ (823m).

For a more gentle, meditative experience, try the incredible nature tours through the _Black River Gorges National Park_. In the southwest, especially around Chamarel, you will be astounded by the diversity of the trails, passing sugar-cane fields, coffee plantations and the _Cascade Chamarel_ waterfall. In the east of the island, you can enjoy a gentle tour in the _Vallée de Ferney_ or through the _Domaine de l'Etoile_ nature reserve.

A guide is a good idea for longer hikes or for mountain climbing as it is easy to slip, especially on rough or damp terrain. Also, it is not always easy to keep your bearings. And don't forget that you will tire more quickly when hiking or climbing during the hot and humid months between December and March. The _Forestry Service (Facebook: Mauritius Forestry)_ provides tips for tours. Guided walks are organised in the west of the island by _Yanature (tel. 52 51 40 50 | trekking mauritius.com)_ and in the south by _Horazi (tel. 58 14 88 05 | venture mauritius.com). Vertical World (tel. 6 97 54 30 | verticalworldltd.com)_ offers climbing tours in Curepipe.

## PARAGLIDING

German paraglider _Hans Joachim (tel. 58 52 81 61 | paraglidingmauritius. com)_ will be more than happy to take you on a tandem flight. Revel in the silence beneath the clouds and enjoy the views over island and ocean. You can choose between several different routes: by the sea, over sugar-cane fields, or over the peaks of Pieter Both or Le Morne. Hans flies daily, depending on weather conditions; make sure to call a good 48 hours in advance.

## RIDING

At Mont Choisy in the Grand Baie area there are several options for guided horse-riding trips at the _Horse Riding Delights (tel. 2 65 61 59)_ farm. Alternatively, you can trot off on your own over their 750 hectares of land. You can ride on the beach at Le Morne, where _Haras du Morne (tel. 59 08 90 54 | harasdumorne.com)_ organises hacks.

Also in the south, near Souillac, you can explore nature on former racehorses spending their well-deserved retirement at _Centre Equestre De Riambel (tel. 57 29 45 72 | beach horseridingmauritius.com)_. Rides on the beach are also an option in the west of the island in Flic en Flac at the _Pearle Beach (pearlebeachresort.com)_ resort, or in the east on the beach of the _Tropical Attitude Hotel (short.travel/ mau22)_.

If you want to go one step further, with a horse-riding holiday, opt for the _Maritim Resort & Spa (Balaclava | Terre Rouge | tel. 2 04 10 00 | short. travel/12)_ on the northwest coast. The hotel complex includes a riding stable! For something special, experienced riders are able to swim in the sea with their horses. Rides on the 25-hectare grounds and lessons in the hotel's own riding arena, meanwhile, are suitable for all levels.

## SAILING

Most hotels rent sailing boats and small sailing catamarans (Hobie Cats). The best time to sail is between June and September, when a stiff breeze blows in, especially on the east coast. Take lessons at *Wildwind Adventures (tel. 54 76 41 04 | wildwind-adventures. mu)* in Mont Choisy in the northwest of the island. There are also plenty of sailing trips to choose from, whether you fancy an overnight catamaran cruise along the west coast or a full-day boat trip to Île aux Bénitiers *(short. travel/mau17)*.

## STAND-UP PADDLING

The turquoise lagoons and warm waters are practically begging you to try SUP! On the board, you can discover coves, coastlines or beautiful reefs with colourful fish. Rental companies should provide suitable shoes and life jackets. You'll find providers at all major beaches, such as Preneuse or Anse La Raie.

## SURFING & KITESURFING

Head out across the lagoons and over the reef between June and September for gigantic waves. In Mauritius, the best time for kitesurfing is during the winter months when the southeasterly trade winds blow the strongest. The best kitesurfing spots are: Belle Mare and Palmar, Poste Lafayette, Cap Malheureux, Bel Ombre and Le Morne. Almost all hotels provide boards for free, and courses are also available.

## TENNIS

Public tarmacked tennis courts are located along the coastal road between Péreybère and Cap Malheureux. All the large hotels, as well as some of the smaller ones, have floodlit tennis courts – free, of course, for hotel guests!

## UNDERWATER WALK

You put on a glass helmet that supplies you with oxygen, head down to a depth of between 3m and 4m and walk in slow motion along the seabed, surrounded by magically colourful fish. A boat from *Captain Nemo's Undersea Walk (tel. 2 63 78 19)* leaves from Belle Mare to special spots with fine, sandy seabeds and coral stacks. Other providers are also available, in Grand Baie, for example.

Diving and snorkelling are offered almost everywhere along the coast

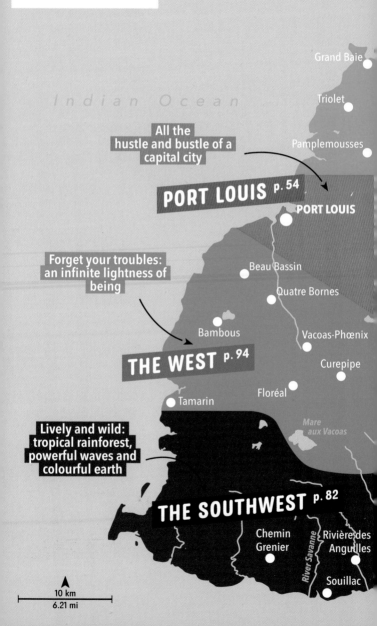

Indian Ocean

Grand Baie

Triolet

Pamplemousses

**All the hustle and bustle of a capital city**

**PORT LOUIS** p. 54

**PORT LOUIS**

Beau Bassin

Quatre Bornes

**Forget your troubles: an infinite lightness of being**

Bambous

Vacoas-Phœnix

Curepipe

**THE WEST** p. 94

Floréal

Tamarin

Mare aux Vacoas

**Lively and wild: tropical rainforest, powerful waves and colourful earth**

**THE SOUTHWEST** p. 82

Chemin Grenier

River Savanne

Rivière des Anguilles

Souillac

10 km
6.21 mi

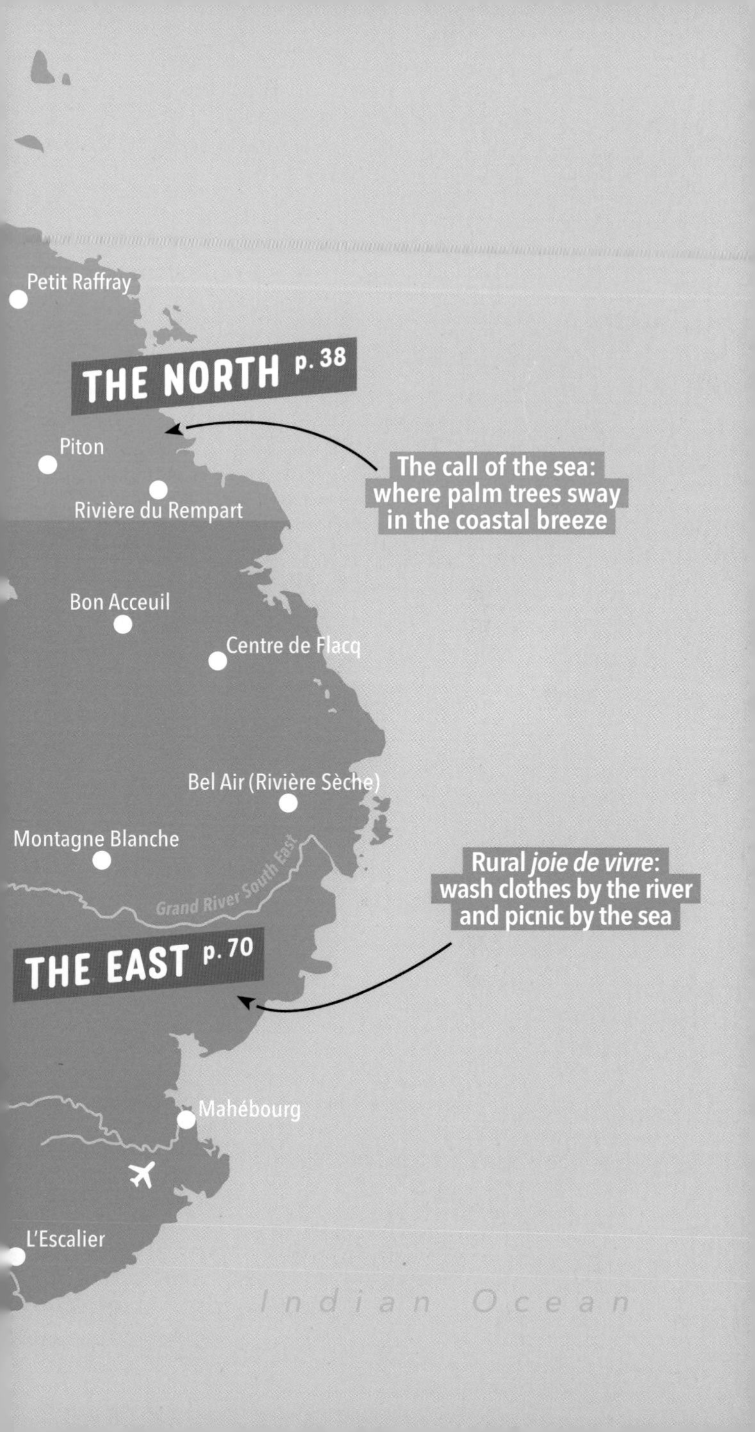

Petit Raffray

THE NORTH p. 38

Piton

Rivière du Rempart

The call of the sea:
where palm trees sway
in the coastal breeze

Bon Acceuil

Centre de Flacq

Bel Air (Rivière Sèche)

Montagne Blanche

Grand River South East

Rural *joie de vivre*:
wash clothes by the river
and picnic by the sea

THE EAST p. 70

Mahébourg

L'Escalier

Indian Ocean

# THE NORTH

## A BEACH PARADISE

The north is the most developed region for the tourist industry. This is most likely due to the weather: low levels of rainfall and wind but lots of sun. There isn't a more beautiful place on Mauritius to watch the sun set into the sea.

The holiday centres of Trou aux Biches and Grand Baie are relatively close to each other, and both are home to top restaurants, bars, cafes and cinemas, as well as boutiques and souvenir shops, marinas, charming family guesthouses and luxurious hotels.

Sun, sand and palm trees: Grand Baie is the epitome of the tropical beach resort

Outside those coastal areas, the region is fairly sparsely populated. A main road runs through Triolet, Goodlands and Pamplemousses, dotted with a few shops and houses. Huge sugar-cane fields stretch between the villages, creating a metre-high green landscape between March and September, which suddenly looks bare and barren after the harvest, but then offers views all the way to the ocean.

The region is defined by colour: bright temples, white churches, pink villas and flame trees that glow crimson-red at the turn of the year.

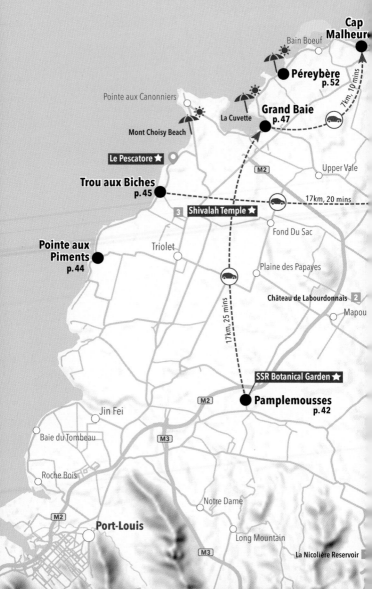

INDIAN OCEAN

Coin de Mire

The Islands in the North ★

Cap Malheur

Bain Boeuf

Péreybère
p. 52

Pointe aux Canonniers

La Cuvette

Grand Baie
p. 47

7km, 10 mins

Mont Choisy Beach

Le Pescatore ★

Upper Vale

M2

Trou aux Biches
p. 45

17km, 20 mins

3 Shivalah Temple ★

Fond Du Sac

Pointe aux Piments
p. 44

Triolet

Plaine des Papayes

Château de Labourdonnais 2

Mapou

17km, 25 mins

SSR Botanical Garden ★

M2

Pamplemousses
p. 42

Jin Fei

Baie du Tombeau

M3

Roche Bois

Notre Dame

M2

Port-Louis

Long Mountain

M3

La Nicolière Reservoir

## MARCO POLO HIGHLIGHTS

★ **SSR BOTANICAL GARDEN**
A heavenly sea of trees and blossoms,
famous for its giant water lilies ➤ p. 42

★ **LE PESCATORE**
This gourmet restaurant on the fishing
harbour at Trou aux Biches is a favourite
with honeymooners and romance
seekers ➤ p. 46

★ **SHIVALAH TEMPLE**
Marvel at the size and splendour of this
colourful Hindu temple ➤ p. 47

★ **THE ISLANDS IN THE NORTH**
Relax with snacks and cocktails on board
your yacht, then stop off at a small
island to swim, snorkel and sunbathe.
Perfection! ➤ p. 49

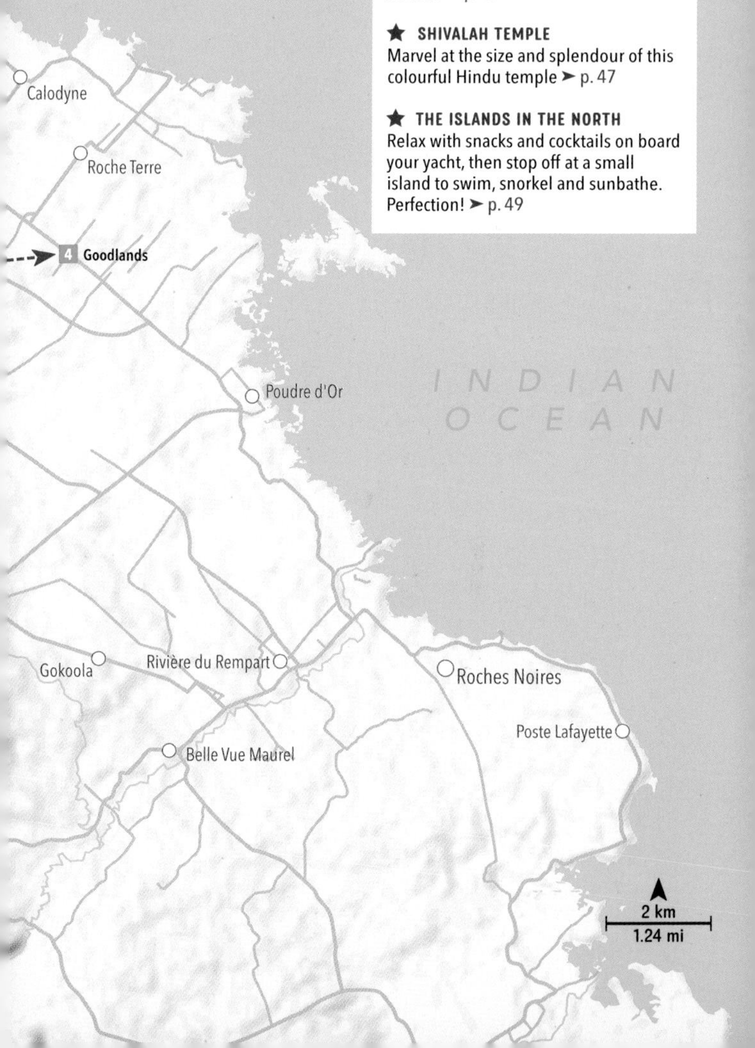

Calodyne

Roche Terre

⟶ 4 Goodlands

Poudre d'Or

INDIAN
OCEAN

Gokoola

Rivière du Rempart

Roches Noires

Poste Lafayette

Belle Vue Maurel

2 km
1.24 mi

# PAMPLE-MOUSSES

*(□ E5)* **Were it not for the Botanical Garden, Pamplemousses would hardly be worth a mention.**

That said, the provincial town is still home to oldest church on the island, the largest public hospital on the island, and a lively main street with various shops and fast-food outlets.

## SIGHTSEEING

### L'AVENTURE DU SUCRE

This museum is just plain good fun. Large display boards and exhibits like old ox carts or rum kettles tell the story of cane sugar, its cultivation and processing, and rum production. And you will learn something new, too: not all sugar is the same, and there are sweet tastings that delve into the finest of nuances. A fantastic restaurant and beautiful boutique with high-quality souvenirs, honey, sugar and excellent rum round off the offer. *Daily 10am–4pm | admission 525 rupees | Beau Plan | aventuredusucre. com | ⊙ 1½ hrs*

**INSIDER TIP**
**Sweet nuances**

### CHURCH OF ST FRANÇOIS D'ASSISE

This church, with its simple façade and impressive wooden beams in the nave, was the first to be built on the island (1756). In fact, it was even here before the town itself. The cemetery is

also worth a look. You'll see many old graves like that of Abbé Buonavita, who was Napoleon's priest during his exile on St Helena.

### SIR SEEWOOSAGUR RAMGOOLAM BOTANICAL GARDEN ★

It's pretty certain that back in 1756, Governor Mahé de Labourdonnais would never have dreamed that his vegetable garden would one day become the Royal Botanical Garden and Mauritius's principal place of interest. Huge water lilies, liverwort trees and palms that blossom only once in every 30 years make for a tropical paradise. Take a guided tour to learn about this wonderful garden, with its enclosure of ponderous giant tortoises and old sugar mill. As if that weren't enough, there's also Mon Plaisir, a colonial villa dating from 1777, and a wrought iron entrance gate that was displayed and won first prize at the International Exhibition in London in 1862. *Daily 8.30am–5.30pm | admission 200 rupees, 1 hr tour 50 rupees | ⊙ 2 hrs*

## EATING & DRINKING

### CAFÉ WIENER WALZER (VALSE DE VIENNE)

If you are on the hunt for some contrast after a visit to the Botanical Gardens, why not visit this Austrian-style garden café? You can enjoy the likes of a chicken curry before diving into a slice of *sachertorte* or bowl of ice cream. *Daily 9am–5pm | Powder Mill Road, behind the church | tel. 2 43 84*

65 | *Facebook: Wiener Walzer Cafe –
Valse de Vienne Cafe* | €-€€

### LE FANGOURIN
Excellent Creole cuisine and you get to
sit outside in the heart of the park next
to the sugar museum. Take the opportunity to sample the chef's impressive
cocktails. *Daily 9am–4.30pm | Royal
Road | tel. 2 43 79 00 | le-fangourin.
restaurant.mu | €€*

## SHOPPING

### MARITIME MODELS CO. LTD.
The employees in this store will gladly
tell you about the production of scale-
model sailing boats like the Gorch
Fock, Bounty or Wasa, which can be
purchased here. You can buy a variety
of models at the Commercial Centre in
Pamplemousses too. *Mon–Sat 9am–
4pm | Royal Road, behind the SSR
Botanical Garden*

# AROUND PAMPLE-MOUSSES

### 1 LA NICOLIÈRE RESERVOIR
*8km from Pamplemousses, 10 mins
by car on the A2 and B49*
The La Nicolière drinking water reservoir is near Villebague. This trip offers
a beautiful drive into the island's
heartland along an ascending road
lined with conifers before you eventu-
ally reach a wonderful viewpoint

Towering plants in the Botanical Garden

overlooking the reservoir. From there,
you can see the all the way to the
east and west coasts.
Perhaps you'll even
see monkeys gawping
at the visitors' reflec-
tions in the water. *E6*

**INSIDER TIP
Monkey fun**

Colonial life from the mid-19th century is on show at Château de Labourdonnais

### 2 CHÂTEAU DE LABOURDONNAIS

*8km from Pamplemousses, 10 mins by car on the B11*

This *château* is located in the middle of a park in the town of Mapou. The building, constructed in 1859, is still family-owned. The garden was also laid out in the mid 19th century and is a tropical dream with its magnificent arboretum, which includes a 100-year-old mango, plus nutmeg and clove trees. There's also a rum distillery and bar on site, and a restaurant *(€€–€€€)* that offers menus from colonial times. *Daily 9am–4pm | tel. 2 66 30 07 | domainedelabourdonnais.com | ⏱ 2 hrs | ▱ E5*

# POINTE AUX PIMENTS

*(▱ D5)* **Several luxury hotels sit along the fine sandy beaches around Pointe aux Piments and stretching right down to the Bay of Balaclava.**

There are wonderful spots for snorkelling at the mouth of the *Rivière Citron* in the *Baie aux Tortues (Turtle Bay)*. The coral reef is easily reachable and is not far from the beach. Aside from the hotels, there's hardly any infrastructure here at all.

## EATING & DRINKING

### SOLEIL COUCHANT

The menu includes inexpensive and good curry dishes and delicacies. Crab, shrimp and grilled fish are also served, and there's a sea view. *Daily | Royal Road | tel. 2 61 67 86 | €*

### VERANDA POINTE AUX BICHES ☎

Chic ambience and excellent local and international cuisine at this beachfront resort. It's also child-friendly with something for the little ones to eat while they romp around, such as freshly fried samosas or *dholl puri* (savoury pancakes filled with lentils). Two restaurants and a bar. *Daily 7–10pm, bar also open during the day | between Pointe aux Piments and Trou aux Biches | tel. 2 65 59 01 | veranda-resorts.com | €€*

## SPORT & ACTIVITIES

### YEMAYA ADVENTURES

Experience the intensity of nature through adventure and sporting challenges on tours from sports instructor and cycling champion Patrick Haberland. His agency is named after the African goddess and bringer of luck Yemaya. And whether you're hiking, mountain biking or kayaking, Patrick is usually there in person. But watch out – his enthusiasm for the island is contagious! From *Le Pouce* you'll get a wonderful view of the north of the island. *Tel. 57 52 00 46 | yemayaadventures.com*

**IDER TIP**
**Adventure and enthusiasm**

## WELLNESS

### VED HOLISTIC CARE CENTER

An unassuming and laid-back ambience with experts offering a treasure trove of Ayurvedic treatments. The eight-handed massage *(1 hr, 3,500 rupees)* is a wellness highlight, especially for head and neck pain. *Mon–Sat 8.30am–5.30pm, Sun 9am–noon | Royal Road, opposite the Social Welfare Centre | Triolet | tel. 2 61 72 71 | ayurvedicmassagemauritius.com/web*

# TROU AUX BICHES

*(f D4)* **When people talk about Trou aux Biches, they're thinking less about the small village and more about its beautiful white beach.**

Especially at weekends, it's the destination for thousands of fun-seekers, particularly families. The gleaming white beach may once have seemed glamorous but, compared with those with more modern facilities, the ambience is now disappointing. Still, the 4km-long stretch of sand and the turquoise blue water make up for a lot!

## EATING & DRINKING

### LA MARMITE MAURICIENNE

Simple restaurant with a cosy atmosphere. Creole cuisine, fish and seafood, Mauritian. *Daily noon–2pm and 5–10pm | Trou Aux Biches Road | tel. 2 65 76 04 | marmiteresto.com | €–€€*

### LE PESCATORE ★

Guests sit on a wooden veranda in an elegant atmosphere right by the pier and enjoy the view of the sea and the boats swaying in the breeze. The finest Creole cuisine, and the best gourmet restaurant on the island. Reservations required. *Mon–Sat noon–2pm, 7–10pm | Coastal Road | tel. 2 65 63 37 | lepescatore.com | €€€*

## SPORT & ACTIVITIES

### BLUE SAFARI SUBMARINE 🐠

Guided dives: the *Blue Safari* submarine dives down to the coral reefs to a depth of up to 40m. The glass enclosure provides a 360-degree view of fish, turtles and shipwrecks. The experience is particularly intense when the engine is briefly switched off. Or you can chose a trip with a sub scooter, a small underwater vehicle that you control yourself and take into the shallow waters down to a maximum of around 3m (for those over 12 years old only). *Daily 8–5pm | submarine 5,000 rupees (approx. £93), scooter for 2 people 7,000 rupees (approx. £130) | near Le Pescatore | tel. 2 63 33 33 | blue-safari.com*

### BLUE WATER DIVING CENTER

Owner Hugue Vitry offers tours to old shipwrecks and to the *Whale Rock sea cliffs*, plus adventurous night diving trips

**INSIDER TIP**
**Shark tank**

and visits to the *Shark's Pit*, where sharks will swim all around you while you're protected in a tank. A dive costs about 3,650 rupees (approx. £70), including equipment. *Royal Road | tel. 2 65 71 86 | bluewaterdivingcenter.com*

### HORSE RIDING DELIGHTS

Explore the lush vegetation in Mont Choisy Leisure Park on horseback, riding along tree-lined avenues and discovering small lakes along the paths. A visit to the film-worthy Colonial House will take you on a trip back into the past. *Daily 8am or 3pm | horseback ride with refreshments 2,100 rupees (approx. £40 | near Mont Choisy beach | tel. 2 65 61 59 | horseridingdelights.com | ⏱ approx. 1½ hrs*

## BEACHES

### MONT CHOISY BEACH 🏖

This beautiful, long beach is the stuff of dreams, with shady trees and a few snack stops. It's rarely crowded during the week but the locals descend at weekends for a picnic. *D4*

# AROUND TROU AUX BICHES

### 3 SHIVALAH TEMPLE ★

*1km from Trou aux Biches / 5 mins by car*

Things don't get much more colourful than this! The largest temple complex in Mauritius is located at the northern end of *Triolet*. Its vibrant splendour is mostly due to the various painted deities, ornaments and floral patterns. Erected in 1891 in honour of the gods Shiva, Krishna, Vishnu, Muruga, Brahma and Ganesha, the temple is a real sanctuary for Hindus on Mauritius. During the annual *Thaipoosam Cavadee* festival in January/February, thousands of believers make the pilgrimage to the complex. Be prepared, you'll have to take your shoes off to enter the building. *Shivalah Road | ⫝̸ D4*

# GRAND BAIE

*(⫝̸ E4)* **Grand Baie is generally regarded as the Côte d'Azur of Mauritius. It is a top destination if you want to hit the bars, dance the night away, make new friends or just have fun.**

There's plenty going on in the daytime, too. If you don't fancy hopping on a catamaran, cruising through the beautiful bays or heading out on a water ski, you can instead enjoy the colourful spectacle by the ⚑ *harbour* at noon, when the fishermen come back with their catch, which they sell directly from the quay next to the water sports centre. If you fancy a stroll

There's always plenty of activity on the beach at Trou aux Biches

on dry land, take a walk to the coastal road where you will find plenty of shops, snack bars and galleries.

## EATING & DRINKING

Those smells! Sample your way through the many ⚑ street food stalls around the town and on the promenade for your very own mini culinary tour of the Creole cuisine of Mauritius. You'll find fresh Indian flatbread with vegetables as well as fried pastry samosas filled with vegetables, fish or chicken.

### CAFÉ MÜLLER

Brunch in Café Müller every Saturday from 8am to 11am is cheap (around 500 rupees) and delicious. It's popular, so it's best to book. As the name suggests, this is a German-run café. *Sept–June Thur–Sat 8am–5pm | Royal Road | tel. 2 63 52 30 | Facebook: Café Müller Mauritius*

### LE CAPITAINE

**INSIDER TIP**
**Fine fish with a view**

Top-class cuisine with a wide range of fresh fish, lobster, langoustines and mussels to choose from, all beautifully presented. A true taste sensation and the luxury of a view over the bay only adds to the experience. *Tue–Sun | Royal Road | tel. 52 53 55 05 | lecapitaine.mu | €€–€€€*

### COCOLOKO RESTAURANT

Enjoy international cuisine (burgers, pizza, pasta, fish and meat dishes) in a tropical garden under the coconut trees. Plus delicious cocktails! *Daily |*

*Royal Road | tel. 2 63 12 41 | cocoloko. net | €€*

### THE GOURMET GRILL

One of the best restaurants on the island. The menu offers grilled fish and meat specialities alongside spicy vegetarian dishes for non-meat-eaters. The Banana Beach Club next door provides the musical setting. *Mon–Sat from 4pm | Royal Road | tel. 52 52 08 97 | bananabeachclub.com | €€–€€€*

### RESTAURANT COOLEN CHEZ RAM

This friendly family restaurant serves up fresh fish and spicy Creole cuisine, at a very reasonable price and with a lovely team. *Thur–Tue noon–2pm, 6.30–10pm | Royal Road | tel. 2 63 85 69 | chezram.com | €*

## SHOPPING

The boutiques along Royal Road are particularly aimed at younger shoppers. They have a huge selection of t-shirts, trousers, dresses, hats and scarves to get you in the holiday mood.

### BAZAR DE GRAND BAIE

Tucked away in the narrow streets near the La Jonque Restaurant is this small market that sells fruit, vegetables, clothes and fashion accessories. *Mon–Sat 6am–6pm | Racket Road | Facebook: Grand Baie Bazaar*

### LA CROISETTE GRAND BAIE

Find anything you could imagine here with 80 shops, 24 restaurants, play areas for the kids, mini-golf, an internet café, pharmacy and supermarket

Non-divers can take a stroll along the seabed

to choose from. *Mon–Thur 9.30am–7.30pm, Fri/Sat 9.30am–8.30pm | Chemin Vingt Pieds | gblc.mu*

### SUNSET BOULEVARD
This shopping arcade has a great ambience. Its selection of first-class shops mainly sell fashion, but you can also find home accessories and creative trinkets like lace cushions or tasselled bags. *Mon–Sat 9.30am–6pm | Coastal Road | Facebook: Sunset Boulevard Mauritius*

**INSIDER TIP**
**Island style for your home**

## SPORT & ACTIVITIES

### DIVING
Several diving centres organise excursions to dive sites in the north, such as *Pointe Vacoas, Aquarium* and *Flat Island*. Some centres belong to the *Mauritian Scuba Diving Association*

*(msda.mu/diving-center-region/nord)*, but hotel diving schools also organise excursions.

### THE ISLANDS IN THE NORTH ★
A cruise on a catamaran along the steep coast of *Coin de Mire (▢ E2–3)* is a dream, and not just for sailors. You'll drop anchor at the *Île Plate (Flat Island | ▢ F1–2)* and *Îlot Gabriel (▢ O)*, which boast white beaches, and there's enough time for snorkelling and a stroll across the island. After about two hours you will return to the boat where a barbecue is served. *Croisières Australes (daily 9am–5pm | price incl. meals from 2,600 rupees, approx. £49 | tel. 2 02 66 60 | croisieres-australes.com).*

### SOLAR UNDER SEA WALK 🌴
Not even your hairstyle will suffer when you are walking at three or four metres under the sea to feed the fish

with an oxygen helmet on your head. *Mon–Sat 9am–5pm | 500 rupees for 20 mins | Royal Coastal Road, near Banana Beach Club and State Bank | tel. 52 53 69 61 | underseawalk.mu*

### SPORTFISHER
Whether it's dorado, tuna or marlin, you're almost guaranteed a catch on one of Sportfisher's fishing trips thanks to the team's professionalism. You'll be most successful between November and March. *Daily | half day speed-boat fishing approx. 23,410 rupees (approx. £435) | tel. 2 63 83 58 | sportfisher.mu*

Robinson Crusoe vibes on Îlot Gabriel

## BEACHES

The bay at Grand Baie is full of ships. You can only swim from hotel beaches and from the popular small beach *La Cuvette*. Wide, sandy beaches are located to the north and south of the city, *on the road to Péreybère (  E3)* and at the *Pointe aux Canonniers (10–15 mins by bus |   D3)*. At the weekend, the Mauritians meet here to swim, picnic and party. ⚑ Young or old, people of all ages sing and dance to traditional sega music. Why not join them!

### LA CUVETTE 🌴
Look out for this beautiful little bay on the way from Grand Baie to Péreybère. The fine sandy beach has market stalls and sun-loungers and parasols to hire, but it's not overcrowded. *10 minute walk from the centre of Grand Baie |   E4*

## WELLNESS

### SHANTIGIRI AYURVEDA SPA
Wellness centre with Ayurvedic massages and treatments, such as Abhyangam, an hour-long massage to raise your count of white blood cells and antibodies, improving well-being and resistance. *Mon–Sat 9am–6pm | Suryamukhi Road | tel. 2 90 21 61 | shantigiriayurvedaspa.com*

## NIGHTLIFE

Bars and clubs in Grand Baie stay open late into the night and attract large crowds. In addition to the venues listed below, popular meeting spots include the *Banana Café (Facebook: Banana Beach Club Mauritius)* and the *Cocoloko Bar (coco loko.net)*, with its tropical garden and large selection of house cocktails.

### BEACH HOUSE
The ideal spot for sunsets by the beach with a view out over the boats. As well as a fantastic selection of wines, there is pizza, pasta and barbecued food. The restaurant and bar are popular with both locals and tourists. *Daily until 10.30pm | Royal Road | thebeach house.mu*

### COCOCHILL RESTAURANT
Now this is a holiday! Relax by the largest swimming pool in the archipelago with cocktails and tapas. The atmosphere is best at dusk when the colourful lights shine. *Wed–Mon 11am–11pm | Royal Road, Pointe aux Cannoniers | coco-chill.com*

### INSOMNIA NIGHT CLUB
One of the most popular clubs in town with hip-hop, techno, dance and disco on the musical agenda. *Fri/Sat 11pm–5am | Coastal Road | insomnia.mu*

### SAFARI BAR
The biggest and one of the most popular nightclubs on the island, where you can dance the night away over two floors. *Daily from 10pm | Royal Road | Facebook: SafaribarMauritius*

# AROUND GRAND BAIE

### 4 GOODLANDS
*11km from Grand Baie / 15 mins by car on the B12*

Goodlands is a typical, small Mauritian town with a lot of traffic. Only the small side streets branching off into residential areas are more peaceful. Shops' goods spill out onto the pavements, and a busy *fruit and vegetable market* is held here *on the town's eastern outskirts*. In addition, textiles are sold on Wednesday and Saturday mornings, and on Tuesdays and Fridays. The market is not busy with tourists and has a lively atmosphere.

Across from the market is the *Historic Marine* factory *(Mon–Fri 8.30am–5pm, showroom also open Sat/Sun 9am–noon | free admission | historic-marine.com)*. This workshop has been producing model ships of the highest quality since 1982. You can watch the craftsmen at work with their materials.

A *kayak tour* with *Yemaya Adventures (6 hrs from around £60 | tel. 52 54 32 05 | yemayaadventures.com)* heads for *Île d'Ambre*, through mangrove forests and heading out to sea between small islands. At noon, you'll have a picnic on the island. You'll take a snorkelling break before paddling to the fishing village of *Grand Gaube* and on to *Calodyne*. Excursions start from Goodlands, from where you'll take a minibus to *Saint Antoine*. F4

Notre-Dame Auxiliatrice enjoys a perfect position on the tip of the cape

# PÉREYBÈRE & CAP MALHEUREUX

*(□ E3)* **Colourful beach towels and other souvenirs flutter in the wind outside shops, and nearby, small restaurants offer tables in the shade of the filao trees. The town of Péreybère is quieter and more peaceful than Grand Baie.**

Set around a bay with a beautiful beach, there are a few small, simple hotels, and many apartments offer rooms that are very popular with families, backpackers and young people.

Just a short distance further on lies *Cap Malheureux*, the "Cape of Bad Luck". The coast is rugged and barren here. It's unclear whether the cape gained its name because of the many ships that ran aground, or due to the French defeat by the English nearby, who then advanced on Port Louis. Private villas along the coast unfortunately block the sea view, although you can enjoy a panoramic vista right on the cape from outside the small wooden church, *Notre-Dame*

*Auxiliatrice*, which is visible from a distance thanks to its red roof. In clear weather you can see out over the small islands of *Coin de Mire, Île Plate* and *Île Ronde* with their steep cliffs.

## EATING & DRINKING

### KANACO

Informal, family-run restaurant that serves fresh fish and seafood. Curries are also delicious. *Daily noon–3pm, 6–9.30pm | Mariamen Temple Road | Cap Malheureux | tel. 57 55 41 27 | Facebook: Restaurant Kanaco | €*

### RESTAURANT AMIGO

Despite the restaurant's 50 tables, Amigo manages to provide a peaceful atmosphere for you to enjoy your lobster and other seafood. Mauritian *cari* dishes are also on offer. The wall serves as a rather unusual guestbook, and there are music performances on some evenings. Reservations are recommended. *Mon–Sat 6–10pm, Tue–Sat also noon–3pm | Le Pavillon | Cap Malheureux | tel. 2 62 62 48 | amigo-restaurant.com | €€–€€€*

## SPORT & ACTIVITIES

### WIND & KITESURFING

The *Club Mistral Mauritius* water sports centre *(Royal Road | Cap Malheureux | tel. 52 55 18 50 | Facebook: clubmistralmauritius)* offers lessons in shallow water as well as trips to more challenging, deeper-sea areas. Good spots for kitesurfing include Cap Malheureux, Anse La Raie and Grand Gaube.

## BEACHES

Fine sand meets crystal-clear water: the 🌴 beach at Péreybère is hugely popular with Mauritians and correspondingly lively; on weekdays it's less crowded. There are bars, restaurants and shops, and roving vendors sell ice-cream and sandwiches. If you're on the hunt for somewhere quiet, you only have to walk a bit further up the beach to find a spot where there's hardly anyone.

## WHERE TO SLEEP IN THE NORTH

### THE ULTIMATE IDYLL

Only adults are allowed in the rooms and suites of the island's most romantic hotel, the *Paradise Cove Boutique Hotel (Royal Road | Anse La Raie | tel. 2 04 40 00 | paradisecovehotel.com | €€€)*, which are situated around a man-made lagoon. The absolute tranquillity makes for total relaxation. The lovingly created facilities have colonial-era Indian influences and create a unique oasis for lovers. Guests are offered a wide, generally free programme of activities, from catamaran trips to underwater walks or cycling. You can also borrow a phone free of charge and even make unlimited calls to Europe. Good cuisine, excellent service and wonderful floral decorations in your room complete the picture.

# PORT LOUIS

## BUZZING CREOLE CITY

(🗺 C–D6) Port Louis is Mauritius's capital and the home of its government. Not only does it have endless shopping streets, several museums and modern skyscrapers (as well as plenty of dilapidated wooden huts), but you will see the island in all its diversity in its many churches, pagodas, temples and mosques. Views of the Moka mountains on the horizon, with peaks up to 800m, give a hint of the greenery that lies beyond the city.

Street life in Port Louis

Port Louis was founded in the early 18th century by the French governor Mahé de Labourdonnais. The city has often been destroyed by fires and cyclones, and much of what remains of the colonial architecture is in need of renovation. Only a small but beautiful historic district near Government House has been restored. It is full of commuters, traffic and crowds. Your best bet is to embrace it: go for a coffee in the side streets, and watch the bustle at the harbour. This is pure Mauritius! However, if you find the city too loud, wait until evening to visit.

# PORT LOUIS

Trou Fanfaron Harbour

**18** Aapravasi Ghat

**17** Windmill

**16** Postal Museum

Star Cinema

Goldfinger

Pink Socks Seafront Bar

**Caudan Waterfront ★**

**Central Market ★** **15**

Blue Penny Museum **1**

Café Lux     MCiné

**"Blue Mauritius" ★**

Le Casino

Bissoondoyal Str.

Queen Str.

Queen Elizabeth Str.

John Kennedy Str.

M2

Government House **12**

**Natural History Museum ★** **2**

Street

...r Street     A1

Barracks Street

Jemmapes Street

Brown Sequard

Photography Museum **3**

Le Café de l'Atelier

Le Courtyard Restaurant

Edith Cavell Street

Mère Barthélemy Street

Saint Georges Street

Saint Louis Street

Ternay Street

Volcy Pougnet Street

De Courcy Street

Labourdonnais Street

**Eureka – La Maison Créole ★**

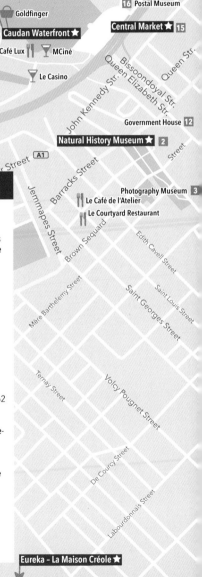

## MARCO POLO HIGHLIGHTS

### ★ "BLUE MAURITIUS"
Particularly valuable because it's not been franked: the world's most famous postage stamp is on display in the Blue Penny Museum ➤ p. 58

### ★ NATURAL HISTORY MUSEUM
Discover what the dodo really looked like ➤ p. 58

### ★ CHAMP DE MARS
Horse-racing on the Champ de Mars: a real carnival atmosphere reigns at the track. Who's your money on? ➤ p. 59

### ★ CENTRAL MARKET
Colourful hustle and bustle around crowded stalls with exotic goods ➤ p. 62

### ★ CAUDAN WATERFRONT
Shop with a view of the sea in this state-of-the-art mall ➤ p. 64, 65

### ★ EUREKA – LA MAISON CRÉOLE
A prime example of Creole architecture from the colonial era. Hoping to move in? Sorry, it's a museum now ➤ p. 68

### ★ KALAISSON TEMPLE
Larger-than-life statues of the gods, fat lions and amazing flowers. Nowhere is more colourful than here! ➤ p. 69

Around 6pm, all of the shops close and everyone disappears. Weekend afternoons are also an option if you prefer a leisurely, quiet wander through Port Louis. Traffic drives on the left, but buses, cars and rattling motorbikes all show little consideration for pedestrians. Despite the day-to-day hustle and bustle, Caudan Waterfront is nice and relaxed. That and the harbour are the only options if you are in search of nightlife.

### WHERE TO START?

**Mahé de Labourdonnais statue** (*□ b2–3*). Whether you drive yourself or take a taxi, it's best to head for the car park (there is a charge) on the Caudan Waterfront. From there, take the underpass to the statue on the market in the old town that commemorates the governor of the East India Company – it's something of a landmark in Port Louis. If you take the bus, get off at the North or South Station.

## SIGHTSEEING

### ■ BLUE PENNY MUSEUM ☂

Good things come in small packages: this holds true both for the building itself as well its two legendary treasures, the *"Red Mauritius"* and – most importantly – the ★ *"Blue Mauritius"*. Admire the pair for ten minutes once an hour from 10.30am. Don't worry too much if you miss the slot: you can still see the museum's copies. As you meander through the rooms, you'll also see ship maps, model ships, old ship instruments and a globe from 1492. There are also boards telling the history of Port Louis and exhibitions on the Mauritian postal service. Last but not least, the museum wouldn't be complete without a statue of Paul and Virginie. Taking photos is prohibited. *Mon–Sat 10am–5pm | admission 245 rupees | Blue Penny Square, Caudan Waterfront | bluepenny museum.com/en | ⏱ 1 hr | □ a2–3*

### ■ NATURAL HISTORY MUSEUM ★ ☂

The museum boasts numerous taxidermy specimens of fish, birds, mammals and reptiles, as well as modern replicas. The whole collection dates back to the century before last and focuses on marine life. That said, nothing here happens without the dodo, and so the extinct bird is also here – for once not as a stuffed creature but as an impressively recreated skeleton in a glass case. The library on the first floor is considered the best archive about the islands of the Indian Ocean. The museum is located on the ground floor of the *Mauritius Institute Building. Mon/Tue, Thu/Fri 9am–4pm, Wed 11am–4pm, Sat 9am–noon | ☛ free admission | Jardin de la Compagnie | short.travel/mau18 | ⏱ 1 hr | □ b3*

> **INSIDER TIP**
> Dead as a dodo

### ■ PHOTOGRAPHY MUSEUM

Formed from the private collection of Tristan Bréville, the museum is like a

Whale exhibits in the Natural History Museum

treasure chest full of old cameras, historic photos and lenses, plus a darkroom with equipment. The scenery used in early studios is also part of the collection. And new exhibits are still being added. Interesting changing exhibitions, too. *Mon–Fri 10am–3pm | admission 300 rupees | end of Rue du Vieux Conseil | musee.photo |* ⏱ *1 hr |* ▥ *c4*

### ☑ CHAMP DE MARS ★ ⚑

Get your glad rags on, add a sun hat and mingle with the vibrant crowd in their Sunday best. Saturdays from March to November are for horses, and the racing starts on the Champ de Mars at 12.30pm. Up to 40,000 people converge here, there's sega music in the background, so why not join the hustle and bustle? Sample the sweet *tarta banana* or hop on the carousel and watch the world go topsy turvy.

As early as 1812, the *Mauritius Turf Club* was organising competitions in this oval racecourse. Back then, the aim was to help the French and British reconcile instead of fighting for supremacy on the island.

A real experience is the *Maiden Cup* in late August when two-year-old racehorses compete for the first time; they are usually pretty cheeky and playful! Why not treat yourself to some real luxury and rent the *Crown Lodge*? The view is fantastic, the champagne flows and you can meet the jockeys *(price incl. transfer, snacks and drinks approx. £165 | To book: tel. 7 29 96 21 | crown-lodge.net). Main entrance D'Estaing*

**INSIDER TIP**
**A (luxury) day at the races**

Street | dates and admission prices: mauritiusturfclub.com | ◻ e–f 5–6

### 5 LAM SOON TIN HOW PAGODA

Three large pagodas stand in the south of Port Louis where most of the Chinese population live. The largest is the *Lam Soon Tin How Pagoda*, right on the southeastern side of the Champ de Mars on Eugène Laurent

### 7 THIEN THANE PAGODA

Only a few streets further on, on Justice Street, stands the *Thien Thane Pagoda*. This tower, with its arched roofs, rises gracefully against the backdrop of the mountains beyond. Inside the octagonal building, you can join the worship. The place buzzes with activity on Chinese holidays. ◻ 0

Queen Victoria is still keeping an eye on proceedings in Government House

Street. It's a gloomy building, but also houses an impressive altar with large statues. ◻ f5

### 6 LIM FAD TEMPLE

The Lim Fad Temple on Volcy Pougnet Street (also called Rue Madame), with its high gate and rich colours, injects a touch of Beijing into an otherwise rather nondescript area. ◻ 0

### 8 FORT ADELAIDE

This fort was built in 1834 on top of the 100m-high *Petite Montagne*. Its architects were the British, who at that time were fearful of French attempts to recapture the island. Luckily, the fort was never called on to fulfil its planned role, instead serving as a barracks for much of its life. The view over the city from this vantage point is excellent. In summer, the courtyard hosts cultural events, while one of the barracks areas is home to a small exhibition about the fort and the dodo. *Admission 50 rupees | Sebastopol Street | ⏱ 1 hr | ⧠ e–f 3–4*

## ⑨ SAINT LOUIS CATHEDRAL

It may be modest as cathedrals go – it looks more like a large church – but the oldest Catholic place of worship on the island looks imposing from the outside, even if it's also rather plain inside. That said, the carved statues are beautiful. Saint Louis is most famous because the remains of the French admiral Mahé de Labourdonnais, the governor of Mauritius from 1734 who helped the colony to prosper, are buried here. In front of the cathedral is a fountain, built in 1786, which for a long time provided the population of the upper part of the city with water from Le Pouce mountain. Behind the church is the 18th-century bishop's residence that looks captivating with its large veranda and beautiful gardens – an oasis of calm in the heart of the busy office district. *Cathedral Square | ⧠ d4*

## ⑩ MARKAZI MOSQUE

This large mosque stands out from afar thanks to its tall minaret. The white building, with arched windows, is built into the row of houses on the busy street. Although it is an eye catcher from outside, it otherwise offers nothing much worth seeing. *Ramgoolam Street/Eugène Laurent Street | ⧠ d3*

## ⑪ CITY THEATRE

This building, with its lovely façade, was built in the 1820s and is thought to be the first theatre in the southern hemisphere. Famous actors and musicians trod the boards here in the 19th century. At the moment, it is closed, but the view from the outside is impressive and the glamour of bygone days still radiates form the theatre. *Jules Koenig Street | ⧠ c3–4*

## ⑫ GOVERNMENT HOUSE

Yes, the traffic is hectic, but it's still worth walking under the royal palms along the imposing *Sookdeo Bissondoyal Street* to Government House. The shade of the large trees is the perfect backdrop to take in the colonial building. The French governors spared no expense when the mansion was built by Mahé de Labourdonnais in 1740 and it was repeatedly extended over time. Today, it is part of the old city centre of Port Louis. The statue of Queen Victoria stands imposingly in the building's inner courtyard; it was erected by the British after their conquest of the island. It is the official address of the Mauritian parliament, which gathers in an extension. Visitors are sadly not admitted. *Jules Koenig Street | ⧠ c3*

## ⑬ CHINATOWN

This is an interesting district with plenty of small handicraft businesses and shops selling household items, Chinese art, medicine, spices like chilli, dried mushrooms, curry, cheap kitsch and all kinds of tat – interesting to browse but don't forget to barter!

There are a number of good Chinese restaurants here and there's always a wonderful aroma of spicy dishes in the air. Small snack bars offer *mine bouille*, a simple but very popular noodle dish. The narrow streets are always full and there's a permanent hustle and bustle, but people here are friendly and you will feel welcome to stay a while and enjoy the chaos. Many of the houses in this part of town date from the period around 1900. Small shops and craft businesses are located on the ground floor, and people live on the floors above. Most are in need of such extensive renovation that they will now be almost impossible to save, but they convey an idea of what a splendid part of the city this must once have been. *c–d 1–2*

### ▓ JUMMAH MOSQUE

This mosque in Chinatown was built in the mid-19th century and is immediately captivating thanks to its artfully carved front door, dazzling white façade and sumptuous interior designed by Pakistani craftspeople. With its Indo-Islamic style, featuring arches and columns, it looks like a small fairy-tale palace.

**INSIDER TIP**
**Courtyard almond tree**

The mosque's ornately decorated inner courtyard is home to an ancient almond tree. Women and non-Muslim visitors may only visit the atrium, from which you can, however, get a glimpse of the prayer hall. Visitors are expected to cover their arms and legs. *Sat–Wed 9.30am–noon, outside prayer times only | Jummah Mosque Street/Royal Street | c–d2*

### ▓ CENTRAL MARKET ★

A wrought-iron gate leads into the covered hall of the *Marché Central (Central Market)* and another world: narrow, crowded aisles, loud voices and steaming cauldrons of meat intermingle with the beguiling scent of vanilla, glowing pyramids of red toffee apples and magnificent parrot fish draped over ice. Of course, there is also a surplus of souvenirs here, many dedicated to the dodo – wooden figurines, t-shirts, bottle openers and the like. Indians offer colourful textiles, Chinese people sell bags of rice and Pakistanis trade exotic flower seeds. Whether you're looking for leather bags, baskets or jewellery, you will be sure to find it here!

**INSIDER TIP**
**Strike a deal**

Make sure that you develop a taste for bartering to avoid regretting an overpriced purchase later. Take your time and linger at the *herb stalls (stall nos. 2, 3 and 460 | harbour entrance)* in the fruit and vegetable market hall. You will find medicinal plants and teas to ward off cellulite, reduce your appetite or treat a headache. Drop in at Jay Mootoosamy's family stall which has been around for over 50 years! If Jay himself isn't there, one of his children or friends will be.

The central market has been on this spot since 1828, although the buildings have burnt down a few times. But the market has always been rebuilt: "You can't kill off a weed," says Jay says with a wink. Despite the many restorations, the façades, cobblestone alleyways and ornate wrought-iron gates still lend a historic feel. *Mon–Sat*

*6.30am–5.30pm, most stalls open at 8am | opposite post office between motorway and Queen Street |* 🗺 *c2*

## 🔢 POSTAL MUSEUM

The museum is housed in what was the General Post Office in the mid-19th century. Today, former wooden telegraph booths, old telephones and extensive stamp collections (although you'll have to head to the *Blue Penny Museum* for the "Red" and "Blue Mauritius") are well worth seeing and a fascinating insight into Mauritian history at the dawn of telecommunications. *Mon–Fri 9.30am–4.30pm, Sat 9.30am–3.30pm | admission 150 rupees | Trunk Road, by the harbour next to the customs house, Waterfront | mauritiuspost.mu/postal-museum |* ⏱ *1 hr |* 🗺 *b2*

## 🔢 WINDMILL 🐷

The windmill on the waterfront was built in 1736 to provide flour for the dockworkers at the harbour. Today it has been turned into a small museum about the history of the surrounding area. From the upper floor windows you can see part of the harbour. *Mon–Fri 10am–noon, 1–3pm | free admission | behind the post office |* ⏱ *30 mins |* 🗺 *b2*

## 🔢 AAPRAVASI GHAT 🐷

After the British abolished slavery in Mauritius in 1834, the state required new workers. These were mainly hired from India, but also from East Africa, China and Southeast Asia. These labourers committed themselves to working in Mauritius for several years. In return, their passage was paid for

Non-Muslim visitors and women can only get as far as the atrium of the Jummah Mosque

and they received room and board in addition to a small salary.

A transit camp was built in the harbour in 1849, which constantly had to be expanded due to the large increase in immigration. The camp remained open until 1923. Over this period, it was the point of arrival for some 450,000 contracted workers from India alone. Although few of the buildings are preserved today, the complex is a UNESCO World Heritage Site, and a visit gives you a feel for the lives of migrant workers in the 19th century. Admission is free. *Mon–Fri 9am–4pm, Sat 9am–noon | Caudan Waterfront, north of the post office at the harbour | aapravasighat.org | ⏱ 1 hr | ▥ c1–2*

## EATING & DRINKING

At lunchtime, 🍴 roving vendors offer quick bites *(roti, gâteaux piments, samosas, soups)* to Mauritians working in Port Louis. For a great and cheap street-food selection, head to the entrance to the market.

### LE CAFÉ DE L'ATELIER 😎

If you're creatively inclined, treat yourself to a delicious sandwich or Creole snack at the café and capture your artistic endeavours on paper at the same time. Located in a small side street, the café is a creative oasis with a pleasant atmosphere. The tools you need are already on the table – pencils and paper! There is an extensive library on the mezzanine with shelves full of books by Mauritian authors. *Mon–Fri 9am–4.30pm | 12 Rue St Louis | tel. 2 08 28 16 | €€ | ▥ b4*

### CAFÉ LUX

Stylish branch of the Mauritian coffee shop chain. The options at the cake counter are temptingly good and the coffee is great, with various different coffee-based drinks served. *Mon–Sat 9am–6pm | Caudan Waterfront | tel. 2 14 60 26 | cafelux.mu | €€ | ▥ b2*

### CAUDAN WATERFRONT ★

Many fast food outlets, bars, cafés and restaurants are located in the shopping centre at the harbour. The food court is set around a sunny terrace. Here, you'll find Indian and Chinese dishes, grills and Creole snacks. If you've got room for a dessert, the various flavours (vanilla, mango, chocolate or pineapple) of the yoghurt ice-cream at *Simis* are delicious. Or opt for a delicious Siro Pike cocktail at *Soleil Aux Sucres (next to the Blue Penny Museum)*: sugar cane is freshly pressed and the juice refined with lemon, ginger or even rum! Bars are open daily from noon until the late evening. *Marina Quay | caudan.com | €€ | ▥ a2*

**INSIDER TIP**
**Sugar, sugar**

### LE COURTYARD RESTAURANT

Fine cuisine artfully served, rounded off with excellent wines. And if that isn't enough, there's a beautiful courtyard with palm trees and fountains. *Mon–Thur 9am–3.30pm, Fri 9am–8.30pm | Chevreau Street | tel. 2 10 08 10 | le-courtyard.com | ▥ b4*

### RESTAURANT LAI MIN

The oldest and most well-known Chinese restaurant on the island

The exuberant Caudan Waterfront houses shops, restaurants, a cinema and a casino

serves excellent takes on traditional dishes. *Daily 11.30am–2.30pm, 6.30–9.30pm | 58 Royal Road, Chinatown | tel. 2420042 | restaurantlaimin.com | €€ | ⊞ d2*

## SHOPPING

### CAUDAN WATERFRONT ★

This unique promenade opened in 1996 around the Labourdonnais Hotel, on a site where warehouses and port containers once stood. Bartering is the norm here, too, even in these air-conditioned arcades. The many attractions include a casino and a cinema, as well as boutiques, jewellers, shoe shops, terrace restaurants and street food trolleys. In total, there are around 170 shops and 25 restaurants and bars.

At weekends, local families flock to the kilometre-long promenade, enjoying the modern urban setting with its skyscraper backdrop – a contrast for many who live in surrounding villages. The fantastic 🎠 *playground (admission for children 50 rupees)* on the waterfront is particularly popular: its lighthouse and ship are made of wood with ropes, nets and slides, which will help your little ones find their spirit of adventure. Then, in the evenings, the younger crowd trickle in, listening to rap and chilling. 🎸 On weekends bands play outdoor concerts on the Waterfront, taking to the stage between 7pm and 9pm. You might hear almost any genre of music. The musicians are very popular and are

**INSIDER TIP**
**Ship ahoy!**

usually mobbed by the crowd. *Shops Mon–Fri 9.30am–5.30pm, Sat 9.30am–7pm, Sun 9.30am–noon | access via the south roundabout of the M1 urban motorway (secure parking daily 7am–11pm, 30 rupees for 4 hrs) | caudan.com | ▥ a2*

### CORDERIE STREET ☂

On *Corderie Street*, which begins behind the market, there are countless fabric shops of various sizes, with a huge selection. Here you will find cotton, linen, silk and rich fabrics artfully embroidered with pearls and sequins at fantastic prices. The sellers like to spread out their wares in front of you. *Mon–Fri 9.30am–5pm | ▥ c2–3*

Tanzanite gems at Goldfinger

### GOLDFINGER

The choice is yours: how about an exquisite yellow diamond, or perhaps a blue tanzanite in a gold setting? Or would you rather create your own piece of jewellery? Then choose a stone, and one of the Goldfinger designers will help make your vision become reality. Seventy-two hours later, you will have your unique item in your hands. *Mon–Sat 9am–5pm, Sun 9am–noon | Caudan Waterfront | tel. 2 69 09 59 | ▥ a2*

### S.S. PATTEN JEWELLERS

Small shop with a workshop run by the Patten family, an Indian jewellery dynasty who have been running their business for generations. The Pattens make silver bracelets, necklaces and pendants – and also the needles that devotees stick through their flesh during the annual Hindu Thaipoosam Cavadee festival. *Mon–Fri 9am–4pm | Emmanuel Anquetil Street | ▥ d2*

## FESTIVALS

### CHINESE NEW YEAR ⚑

Families come together to mark the occasion in January/February. Eating, celebrations and dancing are the order of the day, while offerings are left in the pagodas. Over in Chinatown there is a big parade and the spirit of the devil is symbolically driven away with firecrackers. The exact date of the festival depends on the Chinese calendar and shifts from year to year.

### PORLWI

Port Louis is decorated with lights for this Mauritian festival in late November/early December. Street music, food stalls, art and performances fill the calendar from 7pm until midnight. The city centre remains free of traffic and shops stay open. *porlwi.com*

## NIGHTLIFE

Port Louis tends to be pretty much deserted after the shops and offices close – except at the harbour and the *Caudan Waterfront*.

### CASINO

You enter the casino through the bow of a lavishly designed replica pirate ship. And the interior keeps the pirate theme going throughout. The ground floor is full of one-armed bandits. Up on the first floor, you can try your luck at roulette, blackjack and poker. *Daily 10am–2am | Caudan Waterfront | caudan.com | ▥ a2*

### CINEMAS

*Star Cinema (3 screens | Le Pavillon | tel. 2 11 68 66 | aucinemastar.com | ▥ a2)* in the *Caudan Waterfront* shows current international films in English- or French-language versions. And if you catch a film on its small Star Premium screen things get downright luxurious: the theatre is equipped with comfortable seats that have cushions and allow audience members to put their feet up. And before the movie starts you are served a drink in the lounge and can order à la carte dishes *(€€–€€€)* that will be served during the film.

And if you have ever dreamed of a whole cinema to yourself, the *MCiné (3 screens | Caudan Waterfront | tel. 4 66 99 99 | short.travel/mau21 | ▥ a2)* is ready to make your dreams come true, with private screenings for couples and groups. Just pick your favourite film from the latest programme and enjoy it with drinks and popcorn. The experience costs 7,900 rupees (approx. £147) for a couple or 9,250 rupees (approx. £172) for groups of up to ten people. Just so you know, proposals are also welcome in this romantically decorated space – and champagne is provided!

### PINK SOCKS SEAFRONT BAR

A great place to chill out to enjoyable lounge music. There are live performances on Friday nights with 🐷 happy hour from 5pm to 7pm. Excellent choice of drinks, especially tropical cocktails, and great service. *Daily 5pm–midnight | Le Suffren Hotel | short.travel/mau19 | ▥ 0*

# AROUND PORT LOUIS

### CHAPELLE SAINTE CROIX

*4km from Port Louis / 15-min bus ride*
Catholic priest Père Laval, a native of France, came to Mauritius as a missionary in 1841. He campaigned, in particular, to help the black population and assisted those affected by

leprosy. He was revered even during his lifetime and after his death on 9 September 1864 it's said that many miracle cures occurred at his grave, which is still visited by many sick people. Père Laval was beatified by Pope John Paul II in 1979. Such a great number of believers were visiting his chapel, which contained his glass coffin, on the anniversary of his death that the original building was extended to create a large, modern church with a giant forecourt. There's an exhibition about the life of this "Apostle of Black People" and you can buy souvenirs.

To visit, it's best to take the bus from the Port Louis North Bus Station to Cité La Cure or Père Laval. It's almost impossible to get there by car. *Church daily 6.30am–6pm, services Sun 6am, 8am, 9.30am, exhibition Mon–Sat 8.30am–noon, 1–4.45pm, Sun 10am–noon, 1–4.15pm | 🐖 free admission | northern outskirts of Port Louis | ⏱ 1 hr | 🔲 D6*

## EUREKA – LA MAISON CRÉOLE ★

*11km from Port Louis / 15 mins by car via the M1*

This colonial villa, located on the southern edge of Port Louis in a large park with a waterfall, is a great example of Creole architecture. It was built in 1836, extended in 1856, and remains beautifully preserved to the present day. Decorated with furniture from the 19th century, the rooms on the ground floor convey an impression of what stately life was like in times past. Photographs from that era are also on display in one of the rooms. In addition, the first floor includes a gallery and a souvenir shop. Creole dishes are served to guests on the veranda *(11am–3pm | approx. 800 rupees | reservation required). Villa Mon–Sat 9am–5pm, Sun 9am–3pm | admission to house, garden and waterfall 300 rupees | Montagne Ory, Moka (route signposted from motorway) | tel. 4 33 84 77 | ⏱ 2 hrs | 🔲 D7*

## OFF TO THE MOUNTAINS

From a distance, the mountains *(🔲 D6)* around Port Louis look absolutely spectacular, but most of the peaks can be reached by relatively easy hiking trails. You do need climbing equipment for some of the highest peaks, however: the *Pieter Both* with a distinctive ball-shaped boulder at the top is around 823m high. It's said that as long as the boulder remains up there, all will be well on the island of Mauritius.

The climb up *Le Pouce* (812m) is considerably more comfortable. The route starts at Sainte Anne Chapel near the Champ de Mars racecourse and takes you through the Vallée du Pouce, where the path is clearly visible. Because of the trail's large height difference, you should set aside a good half day for the entire hike. For walkers, the hiking trail on the 306m-high *Priest's Peak* isn't too difficult.

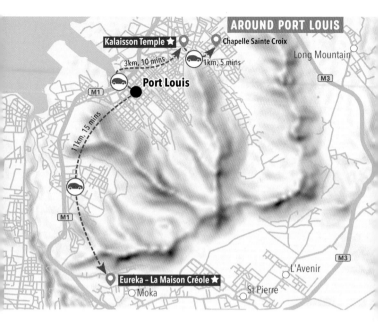

AROUND PORT LOUIS

Kalaisson Temple ★ · Chapelle Sainte Croix
3km, 10 mins · 1km, 5 mins
Long Mountain
M3
Port Louis
M1
11km 15 mins
M1
Eureka – La Maison Créole ★
Moka · L'Avenir · St Pierre
M3

## KALAISSON TEMPLE ★

*3km / 10-min drive north from the city centre*

The Tamil name for this temple is *Sockalingum Meenatchee Ammen Kovil* – it's an amazingly colourful place of worship and a little slice of India on the island. Consecrated in 1860, the Kovil is the single most important religious and spiritual place for the Tamil community in Mauritius. Before visiting, you must leave your shoes at the door because the temple complex may only be entered barefoot. It is best to linger until dusk, when spotlights illuminate the entire complex, making it glow from within. A real goosebump moment!

**IDER TIP**
**Lights and atmosphere!**

In January, the complex is the site of the *Thaipoosam Cavadee Festival* (see p. 121), when devotees pierce their skin with special needles and balance flower-decorated rondels with images of the Hindu god Muruga on their heads. Cavadee is a purification ceremony and days of preparation and fasting precede this immense event. *Daily 8am–6pm | Abercrombie district, near the church of Sainte Croix | ⏱ 1 hr | 🗺 D6*

# THE EAST

## WIND, WAVES AND LOTS OF SUGAR CANE

Pointe Quatre Cocos is the island's easternmost point and is regarded by locals as the end of the world. All in all, it's a bit sleepy! It's a poor area, where residents live off fishing and agriculture, in particular the cultivation of sugar cane, which dates back to the time of the Dutch settlers.

These first inhabitants settled on the flat plains, called *flacq*, and began to cultivate fields very early on. Today, Centre de Flacq, with its beautiful fruit and vegetable market, is the largest town in the east.

The dreamy Île aux Cerfs can be reached by boat from the east coast

The region is also home to magnificent colonial villas where the heirs of the 19th-century sugar barons still live. There are also elegant luxury hotels and incredible beaches between Belle Mare and Trou d'Eau Douce. Mauritian extended families love to gather on the beaches at the weekend for lavish picnics rounded off with sega music and rum.

A light breeze always blows across the land and along the coast, making the sea a paradise for windsurfers and sailors. The region is traversed by the Bambou Mountains, making it good for hikers too.

# THE EAST

Lallmatie

**Poste de Flacq**
p. 80

**Centr**
p. 8

10km
15 mins

Camp Thorel

Espérance

St Julien D'Hotman

Camp de Masque Pave

M3

Dagotiere

Quartier Militaire

Medine Camp de Masque

Bel Etang

Valetta

Providence

Vuillemin

Clemencia

45km, 1 hr

Montagne Blanche

Sebastopol

Belle Rive

Midlands Dam

Domaine de Lagrave  7

Vallée de Ferney ★  6

M2

Montagne du Lion  5

Cluny

St Hubert

Vieux Grand Port  4

Nouvelle France

Morcelement Ferne

Baie de
Grand Port

Rose Belle

Mahébourg
p. 74

Île aux Aigrettes  3

M2

Plaine Magnien

Blue Bay  2

Trois Boutiques

Camp Carol

Camp Diable

L'Escalier

Le Souffleur  1

**Belle Mare** p. 79
○ Quatre Cocos
● Palmar

8 km / 15 mins

**Trou d'Eau Douce** p. 78

**10** Bel Air
xcursion from Bel Air
o Camp de Masque ★

**9** Île aux Cerfs ★

**8** Grande Rivière Sud Est Waterfalls

○ Grand River South-East
○ Quatre Soeurs

○ Grand Sable

○ Bamboux Virieux

INDIAN

OCEAN

## MARCO POLO HIGHLIGHTS

★ **VALLÉE DE FERNEY**
Enjoy the jungle: put on your hiking
boots and head for the nature reserve!
➤ p. 77

★ **ÎLE AUX CERFS**
White sand lapped by crystal-clear water
will have you rubbing your eyes in
disbelief that such beauty exists ➤ p. 79

★ **EXCURSION FROM BEL AIR TO CAMP
DE MASQUE**
After the rain, the air smells like cough
sweets: eucalyptus grows in the valley
between two mountain ranges, not to
mention frangipani, hibiscus and
palms... ➤ p. 81

N
3 km
1.86 mi

Shri Vinayaour Seedalamen temple

# MAHÉBOURG

(□ F–G10) **Former capital Mahébourg (pop. around 20,000) is now a sleepy provincial town. That said, it is still an important centre thanks to its location only 6km from the Sir Seewoosagur Ramgoolam international airport.**

The central point of the town is the bus station. From here you can reach the *Rue Flamant* shopping street, where you can browse the simple shops and street food stalls. A green park is also nearby, and behind it a blue lagoon with a large reef.

## SIGHTSEEING

### CATHEDRAL

*Notre Dame des Anges*, built in 1849 in the English neo-Gothic style, has an impressive ceiling structure with 20 individually carved angels, colourful mosaic windows and a beautiful Madonna figure. It's a place of tranquillity. Sometimes the door to the tower, with a magnificent view over the bay at Grand Port from the top, is open. *Rue Souffleur*

**INSIDER TIP** View from the tower

### NATURAL HISTORY MUSEUM 🐷

A museum in a 300-year-old mansion. The exhibits mostly document the island's colonial past, with a focus on the naval war between France and England. Attractions include wreckage from the battle of 1810, and models of the *St Géran* and one of the trains used on the island from 1864 to 1926. In the garden, several craftspeople have workshops. *Thur–Tue 9am–4pm, Wed 11am–4pm | free admission | Royal Road | short.travel/mau14 | ⏱ 1 hr*

### PARK

Monuments line the promenade with lots of picnic spots and a beautiful view of the ocean. An inconspicuous obelisk commemorates the victims of a shipwreck in 1874. The nearly 6m-high statue of Indian yoga guru Swami Sivananda is more remarkable. *Next to the Bay of Mahébourg*

### TEMPLE

Directly next to the main street, the Tamil temple complex of *Shri*

*Vinayaour Seedalamen* was built in 1856. The complex consists of several large and small temples, and is a yellow colossus with green, red and blue pillars. The façade is on another level, with colourful gods, fighting elephants and various mythical figures. *Daily 6am–noon, 3.30–6pm*

## EATING & DRINKING

### BLUE BAMBOO
A charming Creole garden restaurant with an extensive menu, located on the road to Blue Bay. Wide selection of traditional dishes, spicy curry and great pizza. *Tue–Sun 11.30am–3pm, 6.30–9pm | Pointe d'Esny | tel. 6 31 58 01 | Facebook: Blue Bamboo 2 | €–€€*

### CHEZ PATRICK
Simple restaurant with excellent Chinese and Creole food. Delicious seafood platters. *Wed–Mon 10.30am–2pm, 5–9pm | Route Royale | approx. 200m before the National History Museum from the city centre | tel. 6 31 92 98 | €–€€*

### LE JARDIN DE BEAU VALLON
Part of a small garden hotel. Mauritian specialities, served in the ambience of a colonial house on the edge of a sugar-cane field. *Daily | from the airport, turn right before entering the town | tel. 6 31 28 50 | €€*

### LA VIEILLE ROUGE
This restaurant is very popular with locals because of its fish and seafood cooked according to traditional recipes. Ask about the catch of the day! *Daily 11am–3pm, 6.30–11pm | Rue du Hangard/Rue des Mares, near the church | tel. 57 24 22 86 | €*

## SHOPPING

### BISCUITERIE H. RAULT ☂
Established in 1870, this *biscuiterie* has been passed down from one generation of the family to the next. Today the fourth generation is baking gluten-free biscuits from manioc root from an old recipe and with old tools. There's a bigger selection these days, including vanilla, coconut and chocolate flavours. Try one with a nice cup of tea, coffee or juice for a small extra charge. *Mon–Fri 9am–3pm, Sat 9am–noon | Ville Noire | biscuitmanioc.com*

### MARKET
There is a colourful weekly market every Monday, and people flock here early in the morning. You'll find fruit and veg, spices in every colour of the rainbow, as well as textiles from the local factories, especially t-shirts and summer clothes. There are also stalls for carpets and household appliances. *On the beach promenade, Rue des Hollandais*

## WELLNESS

### BANYAN SPA
The spa at *Preskil Island Resort* is pure relaxation. The only struggle is how to choose between an aromatic bath, a scented massage or an underwater one! Open-air massages are also on offer in a separate area. *Prices on request | Pointe Jérôme | tel. 6 04 10 00 | short.travel/mau20*

## NIGHTLIFE

### SENATOR

The *Senator* casino offers plenty of entertainment for gamblers. Try your luck on the one-armed bandits or at the tables. *Daily 10am–4am | Maida Mount Building, Rue Labourdonnais*

# AROUND MAHÉBOURG

### ◨ LE SOUFFLEUR

*15km from Mahébourg / 20 mins by car on the A12*

When the waves crash against the wild, craggy cliff at this spot, a high jet of water is created along with a whistling sound. There is a hole in the cliff that water has penetrated and now shoots through creating a fountain effect. The waves are high when the sea is rough, and people on the cliff are soaked by the spray. *Access via a cul-de-sac at L'Escalier | ▨ F11*

### ◪ BLUE BAY 🦐

*5km from Mahébourg / 10 mins by car*

Blue Bay, to the south of Mahébourg, is home to one of the many perfect beaches on the east coast. The marine park is ideal for snorkelling – try to spot pipefish, triggerfish, pufferfish and even feeding barracudas up to 1.5m in length! The western part of the park has the most coral. Boat guides will happily show you the best spots for snorkelling. Another great experience is a trip in a glass-bottomed boat

*(1 hr | bookable on the beach).* Surfing is also good here thanks to the calm sea. Head to the visitor centre for information about the unique features of the national park. ▨ G10

### ◫ ÎLE AUX AIGRETTES

*9km from Mahébourg / 10 mins by ferry*

This 25-hectare nature reserve gives you an idea of what Mauritius might have looked like before people arrived. The *Mauritian Wildlife Foundation (mauritian-wildlife.org)* is replanting the original coastal forests of Mauritius here. The island is already home to many species of endangered animals and plants, such as land-dwelling tortoises. At the *Visitor Centre* you can learn about geographical features. Make sure you take sensible shoes, sunscreen and mosquito repellent with you. *Daily, visits only as part of a nature tour | Price incl. ferry on request | Book via local providers or with the Foundation: tel. 6 97 61 17 | Departure from behind the Le Preskil hotel, at "Île aux Aigrettes" car park sign | ⏱ 1½ hrs | ▨ G10*

### ◬ VIEUX GRAND PORT

*10km from Mahébourg / 10 mins by car on the A12*

This was once the most important harbour on the island. Today the defensive complex and the remains of a tower reveal its history. The *Frederik Hendrik Museum* gives an overview *(Mon/Tue, Thu–Sat 9am–4pm, Wed 11am–4pm, Sun 9am–noon | 🐷 free admission | Royal Road | ⏱ 30 mins)* and is stocked with old engravings and archaeological finds. The Dutch

Get to know the inhabitants of Île aux Aigrettes

settlers' graveyard *(Cemetery Road)* is also worth a look. □□ *G9*

### ⑤ MONTAGNE DU LION
*8km from Mahébourg / 10 mins by car on the B28*

If you approach from the south, the Montagne du Lion actually resembles a reclining lion. The tour up to the 480m-high summit begins in the village of Vieux Grand Port. Only experienced hikers should give it a go, since there are a few difficult passages. The view over the sea, which spreads out below in various shades of blue and turquoise, makes the ascent up the mountain unforgettable. □□ *G9*

### ⑥ VALLÉE DE FERNEY ★
*10km from Mahébourg / 10 mins by car on the A12*

The Vallée de Ferney is a forest and wildlife reserve in the Bambou Mountains north of Mahébourg. Guided 3km hikes *(fee 800 rupees)* take 90 minutes and start at the former Ferney sugar plant at 10am and 2pm. The path up the mountain takes you through the forest and past small streams, ivory trees and rare wild plants. This is also the nesting ground for Mauritius kestrels, pink pigeons and tropicbirds.

A transfer from the *visitor centre* to the Vallée leaves every 25 to 30 minutes. From there you can also hike on your own between 10am and 3pm *(fee 600 rupees).* You'll encounter staff members who will point out animals that you might not have spotted on your own.

**INSIDER TIP**
**Discover more wildlife**

Afterwards, pay a visit to the restaurant attached to *Ferney Falaise Rouge (reservations recommended | €€),* which serves meals including venison steak, vegetable curry and fish stew. *Daily 9.30am–4pm | tel. 6 60 19 37 | ferney.mu | ⊞ F9*

### ⁊ DOMAINE DE LAGRAVE
*20km from Mahébourg / 20 mins by car on the A12*

The town of *Bananes* near Midlands Domaine is almost completely hidden behind the sugar cane fields. The nearby forest, with small streams and waterfalls, is home to red deer, monkeys and birds, which you can watch while breathing in the tropical air. There are several guided hikes (⊙ *1.5, 3 or 4.5 hrs | from 300 rupees/pers)* that allow you to explore it. And right in the middle of the countryside the restaurant *Le Daguet (daily 11am–3pm | €€)* serves tasty local cuisine. *Daily 9am–4pm | Eau Bleue, Bananes | tel. 57 32 81 86 | domainedelagrave. mu | ⊞ E9*

# TROU D'EAU DOUCE

(⊞ *H7*) **Trou d'Eau Douce is a fishing village with a small harbour set on a beautiful 3km-long bay with a great 15m-wide ☀ beach.**

From here, boats and catamarans regularly cross over to the Île aux Cerfs on the opposite side. There's a large church built of volcanic rock in the village. The men of the village meet in the tiny *Victoria Square* to play boules.

**LE CAFÉ DES ARTS**

Enjoy the likes of grilled lobster in this restaurant located in a sugar mill dating from 1840, which doubles as a gallery. Dishes from the à la carte menu are served on artfully decorated plates in a room adorned with paintings by Yvette Maniglier, who was Matisse's very last pupil. Reservations required. *Mon–Sat 7.30pm–1am | Old Sugar Mill, Victoria 1840 | tel. 4 80 02 20 | maniglier.com | €€€*

# AROUND TROU D'EAU DOUCE

### ⑧ GRAND RIVIÈRE SUD EST WATERFALLS
*9km from Trou d'Eau Douce / 15 mins by car via the B55 and B27*

Near the town of Beau Champ is the mooring for fishing boats on the Grande Rivière Sud-Est. The anglers are allowed to take holidaymakers to the pretty waterfall in the area. Putter slowly along beside the impressively lush vegetation on the riverbanks and past the coastal villages to the waterfall, which cascades down into the river with tremendous force. *600 rupees for a 20-min tour for up to 6 people, agree price before departing | drive from Beau Champ to Grand Rivière Sud-Est and turn off at "Fisheries Post" | ⊞ H8*

### 9 ÎLE AUX CERFS ★ 🌴

*10km from Trou d'Eau Douce beach / approx. 30 mins by boat*

Pack your goggles, snorkel and fins! A good half-hour boat ride will have you on an island more beautiful than any postcard, where coconut palms fringe a dazzlingly white sandy beach and sunbeams reflect on the ocean. Take a diving tour to see the coral (⏱ *1 hr | price 4,500 rupees, approx £85 | start/ end at the jetty*). The trip will take you once around the island.

**SIDER TIP**
**Underwater paradise**

The water is around 2m deep and you will be treated to the sight of shimmering shoals of light blue fish, plate-sized corals and a view all the way to the seabed. A miniature paradise that feels like it is reserved for you and you alone.

Later, bury your feet in the sand as you sip on ice-cold pineapple juice and enjoy a fruity pizza at the *Sands Bar (daily | Île aux Cerfs Golf Club | tel. 4 02 77 20)*. The island is particularly busy at weekends, when locals gather for a picnic. And this is no case of modest baskets with a few snacks! You'll see people carrying huge pots of curries, rum bottles and hammocks to the beach. Today, only the island's name serves as a reminder of the deer who once peeked out of the thicket here. *Trips daily 9am–5pm | round trip 8,500 rupees (approx. £345) | 🗺 H7–8*

# BELLE MARE

*(🗺 H6)* **Belle Mare takes its name from the area's exceptionally sparkling water.**

The ocean glistens from afar, peeking through the filao trees that line the 🌴 beach, offering shade to visitors. Bathing coves are plentiful here.

Endless green in the protected Vallée de Ferney

Take in the view from the Sagar Shiv Mandir temple

⚐ On weekends, people come together for a picnic on the beach and there's something of a carnival atmosphere, especially along *Plage de Palmar*.

## EATING & DRINKING

### SEASONS RESTAURANT & BAR

This traditional, family-run restaurant might be on the pricier side, but it's classy and just plain good. Whether you opt for spicy tuna salad, crispy samosas or hot lamb curry, for Chinese, Indian or Creole dishes, the quality is always spot on. *Mon–Sat 11am–9pm, Sun until 2pm | on the coastal road opposite the large hotel complex |tel. 4 15 13 50 | orchidvillas.mu/en | €€€*

# CENTRE DE FLACQ & POSTE DE FLACQ

(⫘ G6) **The name "Flacq" is derived from the Dutch word *vlak*, meaning "flat land". Centre de Flacq is in the interior of the country, while Poste de Flacq is 5.5km further to the northeast.**

Poste de Flacq is home to the Hindu temple of *Sagar Shiv Mandir*, located on a tiny peninsula.

Centre de Flacq is a typical small Mauritian town in which a predominantly Indian population lives. The main street is fittingly named *Market Road* and there are shops and stalls as far as the eye can see. The hustle and bustle reaches its height at the *Marché* de Flacq (daily 6am–6.15pm), which takes place around the District Court. The market glitters and smells like a Middle Eastern bazaar, and the air is full of haggling. You can purchase spices like nutmeg and vanilla, as well as fruit and vegetables, at the food market, and the clothes market is also good. Ideally, schedule your market stroll for a Wednesday or Sunday, when it's less crowded.

## EATING & DRINKING

### CHEZ MANUEL

An out-of-the-way Chinese restaurant. The specialities include sweet and sour fish with ginger, pork in honey and venison in chocolate sauce.

*INSIDER TIP*
**The island's sweetest deer**

The portions are generous and Chinese music rounds off the ambience. *Mon–Sat 11am–2.30pm, 6.30–10pm | Royal Road, 8km southwest of Centre de Flacq in St Julien | tel. 4 18 35 99 | Facebook: Chez Manuel Restaurant | €€*

# AROUND CENTRE DE FLACQ

### 🔟 BEL AIR

*8km from Centre de Flacq / 20-min drive*

Romantic little town whose pretty Catholic church of Saint Esprit, with its twin spires, can be seen from afar. This small town south of Centre de Flacq provides the starting point for a nice ★ excursion (12km / 20 mins) around the *Montagne Blanche* (532m), the *Montagne Fayence* (433m) and finally down to *Camp de Masque* (⌂ F7). The coast is some distance away but the air is fresh. During the onward journey to Clemencia, the beauty of nature excels itself, with banana plants, hibiscus, palms, eucalyptus and flowers in all colours. You need to be a little patient when following the town's main and through roads: bikes, mopeds, pedestrians – they're all out and about. ⌂ G7

## WHERE TO SLEEP IN THE EAST

### ECO-CONSCIOUS CAMPING 🏕

One-of-a-kind eco lodge with 12 tents at *Otentic Eco Tent (tel. 59 41 48 88 | otentic.mu | €€€)* in the village of Deux Frères on the banks of the Grande Rivière Sud-Est. Here you will camp in a palm garden with a pool and Creole restaurant. Fancy canoeing, diving, cycling or snorkelling? Take your pick! A shuttle boat will take you to the beach on Île aux Cerfs.

### FOR INDIVIDUALISTS

Creole furniture in a natural stone house with a straw roof and folding shutters as windows. *La Case du Pêcheur (18km north of Mahébourg, behind Bambous Virieux | tel. 6 34 56 75 | lacasedupecheur.com | €)* stands right in the middle of a lagoon, surrounded by oysters and crabs, as well as a mangrove forest.

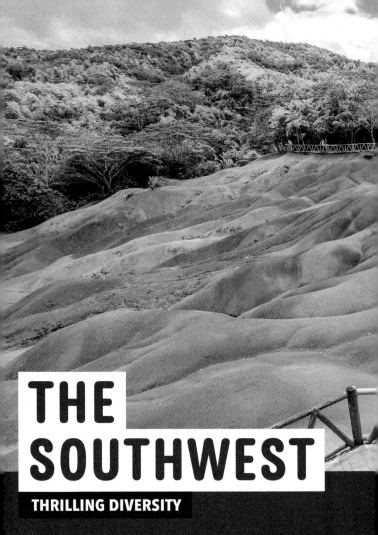

# THE SOUTHWEST

**The southwest remains wild and untouched – the only region on the island that still resembles Mauritius before the settlers landed and began to clear away the jungle.**

Take some trips into the countryside and you'll see steep cliffs, deep gorges, roaring waterfalls and vast lakes. There are also volcanic craters, the colourful Terres des Sept Couleurs and the rugged Morne Brabant. The Black River Peak National Park, a densely vegetated mountain landscape, is unique and home to rare bird species,

How many colours can you see in the Terres des Sept Couleurs?

such as the pink pigeon and Mauritian kestrel. Hike through unspoiled nature and enjoy amazing views, or rest up in one of the fishing villages. People have been settling here since the 19th century: after the abolition of slavery, former slaves came and founded their own villages. Today, the fishing villages are lined up on the narrow strip between the mountains and the sea. Simple wooden huts are nestled next to orchards and vegetable gardens, complete with a scratching ground for chickens and a pasture for a goat or a cow.

# THE SOUTHWEST

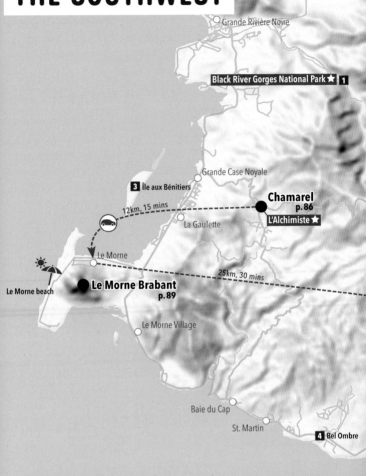

Grande Rivière Noire

**Black River Gorges National Park** ★ **1**

**3** Île aux Bénitiers

Grande Case Noyale

**Chamarel**
**p. 86**
L'Alchimiste ★

12km, 15 mins

La Gaulette

Le Morne

25km, 30 mins

Le Morne beach

**Le Morne Brabant**
**p. 89**

Le Morne Village

Baie du Cap

St. Martin

**4** Bel Ombre

INDIAN OCEAN

## MARCO POLO HIGHLIGHTS

★ **L'ALCHIMISTE**
This restaurant dishes up plates of venison and wild boar followed by its own excellent rum as an after-dinner treat – it's 100 per cent organic ➤ p. 87

★ **BLACK RIVER GORGES NATIONAL PARK**
Put your fitness to the test: climb the Black River Peak in the national park and reap the rewards of an adrenaline rush and a view to die for ➤ p. 87

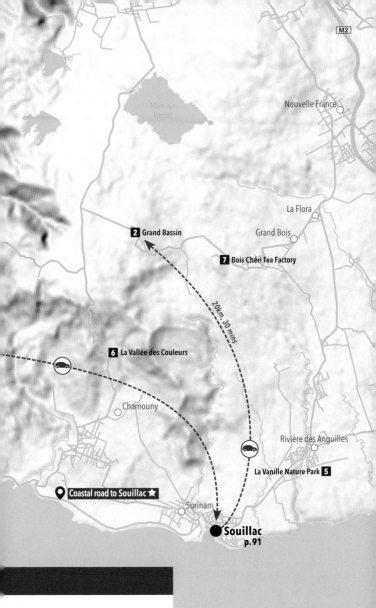

M2

Nouvelle France

La Flora

**2** Grand Bois

**2** Grand Bassin

**7** Bois Chéri Tea Factory

20km, 30 mins

**6** La Vallée des Couleurs

Chamouny

Rivière des Anguilles

La Vanille Nature Park **5**

Coastal road to Souillac ★

Surinam

● **Souillac**
p. 91

★ **COASTAL ROAD TO SOUILLAC**
Creole villages meet bays full of fishing
boats: you'll never lose sight of the
ocean on the journey from Le Morne to
Souillac ➤ p. 91

2 km
1.24 mi

In the south, where the coral reef is interrupted, violent waves crash against the beaches. Unpredictable currents also make swimming dangerous, meaning that there aren't any beach hotels here. In the west, it's the usual scenario, however: calm water, white beaches, filao groves and plenty of holidaymakers.

# CHAMAREL

(□ B10) Surrounded by coffee and sugar plantations is the village of Chamarel, famed for its beautiful surroundings.

Once a year, during the feast of the Assumption on 15 August, this small Creole village of 700 souls turns into a veritable fairground. On this day believers flock to *Sainte Anne Chapel*. With them come vendors and food stalls.

## SIGHTSEEING

### CASCADE CHAMAREL

An avenue of palm trees leads to these 100m-high twin waterfalls. Their capacity actually doubles in the rainy season! You can enjoy the impressive panorama from a viewing platform, looking down on the spray which roars into a densely overgrown, lush green basin. A small path leads to the foot of the waterfalls, where you can take a wonderful dip in the pool. *Combination ticket with Terres des Sept Couleurs 500 rupees | end of the row of houses on Baie du Cap Road*

### CURIOUS CORNER OF CHAMAREL ☎

This house of illusions and mysteries turns the world on its head: in one room you'll be walking on the ceiling of a kitchen, in another you will look like a giant while the other people in the same room appear tiny. Great fun for the whole family and full of surprises. *Daily 9.30am–5pm | admission 475 rupees, children (3–12) 350 rupees | Baie du Cap Road | curiouscornerofchamarel.com | ⏱ 1½ hrs*

### EBONY FOREST ☎

Start by exploring the history of the island, a story full of volanic eruptions and unique, if now extinct, flora and fauna. Next you embark on a guided hike through an ebony forest. There are easy tours *(suitable for children aged 6+)* that are more like walks, but also more strenuous ones like the *Ridgeline Trail (10+)* with fantastic views of the southeast coast. *Daily 9am–5pm | admission 600 rupees, children 400 rupees | Coloured Earth Road | tel. 4 60 30 30 | ebonyforest.com | ⏱ 2 hrs*

### TERRES DES SEPT COULEURS

Charamel is known for its coloured earth. The undulating ground in this park spreads over approximately a hectare. The main colour is a rusty red. Depending on the time of day, the layers of earth can look yellow, orange, blue or even purple, and there's no clear scientific explanation for why this happens. The assumption is that this is probably the coloured remains of the lava layers from different eras. *Park*

Cascade Chamarel is surrounded by tropical greenery

*grounds daily 8.30am–5pm | admission approx. 500 rupees, incl. Cascade Chamarel | end of the row of houses in the Baie du Cap Road | ⏱ 2 hrs*

## EATING & DRINKING

### L'ALCHIMISTE ★

Delicious dishes made from fresh ingredients: the menu includes vegetables they have grown themselves, venison specialities and there is even an afternoon tea with crêpes and pastries. After your meal, why not try one

**SIDER TIP**
**See how rum is made**

of the rum cocktails from the in-house distillery? A meal in the restaurant means you don't have to pay for the guided tour of the distillery. *Mon–Sat until 6pm | Rhumerie de Chamarel | Royal Road | tel. 4 83 49 80 | rhumeriedechamarel. com | €€€*

### LE CHAMAREL

A restaurant with great views spanning the vast countryside to the sea and delicious Mauritian cuisine. The speciality is wild game. After the meal they serve coffee grown on the island. *Daily 9am–6pm | La Crête | tel. 4 83 64 21 | lechamarelrestaurant.com | €€–€€€*

# AROUND CHAMAREL

### 1 BLACK RIVER GORGES NATIONAL PARK ★

*30km from Chamarel / 35 mins by car on the A3*

Several protected nature reserves have been merged together to create this park. At 66km², its landscapes range from the 828m-high *Black River Peak (Piton de la Petite Rivière Noire)*, the island's tallest mountain, to the thick rainforest that grows along the steep slopes of the *Savanne mountains*. Many native plants and endangered species of bird can only be found in this park.

The route through the *Macchabée Tropical Forest* and the *Black River Gorges* is particularly worthwhile, if adventurous. From *Black River Peak* you can see out over the whole island. A hiking path begins near the viewing point. The trail is easy at first but it becomes increasingly demanding. The last part is heavy going and has difficult sections. And watch out! The path is slippery when wet. You're rewarded, however, with a fantastic view of the Indian Ocean and a good bench to take a break. If you don't feel

safe alone in the mountains, Yan is a reliable guide *(tel. 5 78 51 77 | yanature.com)*.

Right in the heart of the national park is the plateau *Plaine Champagne*. A narrow road winds its way through the area, leading to vantage points atop gorges and waterfalls – the most beautiful is the view over the *Black River Waterfall* near Le Pétrin.

**INSIDER TIP**
**Intoxicating!**

The 16km drive from *Le Pétrin* through *Chemin Grenier* to *Rivière des Galets*, past the *Vallée des Couleurs* (p. 93), takes you through forests, and pineapple and vegetable fields.

🐷 Entrance to the national park is free. There are two visitor centres; the larger is in Le Pétrin at the east entrance *(Mon–Fri 7am–4pm, Sat/Sun 9am–5pm)*, the second at the west

Le Morne Brabant looks like a boulder dropped on the coast by giant

entrance in Black River. There is no food or drinking water in the park, so make sure to take sufficient supplies with you. As it often rains in the afternoon, you should visit the area as early in the day as possible. *B–C 9–10*

## ❷ GRAND BASSIN

*17km from Chamarel / 30 mins by car*
Despite what its name might suggest the Grand Bassin is just a small lake. The crater of this extinct volcano is famous for the *Maha Shivaratree* festival. Every spring thousands of Hindu pilgrims visit the holy site in honour of the god Shiva. According to legend, Shiva made a stop in Mauritius with his wife Parvati on a flying ship during his journey to the most beautiful places on earth. While there, he is said to have spilled a few drops of holy water from the Ganges out of an amphora which fell into the Grand Bassin crater. This is how the lake came to be, the legend has it. On its shores there are some small temples and altars, as well as the 35m-tall statues of *Shiva* and *Durga*, which are impossible to miss. *Daily 6am–6pm | free admission | C10*

# LE MORNE BRABANT

(*A10*) **Set on a peninsular, the distinctive Le Morne Brabant mountain (556m) is a real eye-catcher.**

The mountain's connection with the history of the slave trade led to its listing as a UNESCO World Heritage Site. In the 19th century the mountains were the site of a tragic misunderstanding. During French rule, runaway slaves used the slopes of the mountain as a hiding place. When the British abolished slavery, police were sent to the hideouts to inform former slaves of their newfound freedom. However, many believed they had been captured and threw themselves to their deaths. Today, there's a memorial here to commemorate the tragic event. Every year on 1 February, the festival commemorating the abolition of slavery, many come here to have a picnic. Bands play and there's singing and dancing. The gate leading to the path up to Le Morne is open from 7am to 4pm. The ascent and descent take around three hours.

Look out for wildlife in the Bel Ombre nature reserve

Windsurfers and kite surfers converge at the southwest tip of the island on 🌴 Le Morne beach for the best waves at the *One Eye* surf spot.

## EATING & DRINKING

### OCEAN VAGABOND

International cuisine with a Creole touch, including fish curry, king prawns and tuna, but you'll also find Italian pizza made from wafer-thin dough that is well-seasoned and freshly prepared. Good service and a beautiful wooden veranda make for an excellent meal. 🐟 Happy hour is Saturdays from 5pm to 8pm. Booking recommended. *Wed–Mon from 5pm | Royal Road | La Gaulette | tel. 4 51 59 10 | Facebook: oceanvagabondmauritius | €€ | ⌖ A–B 10*

## SPORT & ACTIVITIES

### FLIGHT TO AN UNDERWATER WATERFALL

A helicopter flight over Mauritius is an unforgettable experience. You'll fly over tiny islands in the north, mountains, craters, the national park and the coast. The view from up high of the underwater waterfall is fascinating: it looks

**INSIDER TIP**
**The swallowing sea**

as if the ocean is opening up at the island's southwestern tip and swallowing tonnes of water. But it's an optical illusion. The ocean currents are so strong that they wash the sand away from the coast and fling it into deeper spheres of the ocean, creating the illusion of a waterfall! Tours are provided by *Corail Hélicoptères (daily 8.30am–5pm | 25 mins 12,500 rupees/pers (approx. £233) | SSR Airport Mauritius | tel. 2 61 22 66 | corailhelico-mu.com).*

# AROUND LE MORNE BRABANT

### 🔳 ÎLE AUX BÉNITIERS

*7km from Le Morne Brabant / 10 mins by boat*

A beautiful island set in a turquoise lagoon, with endless white sandy beaches. There are plenty of snorkelling options here, with many coral fields. Boats set off from the Paradis Beachcomber Resort. The farmers on the island were once Mauritius's main suppliers of coconuts. *A10*

### 🔳 BEL OMBRE

*20km from Le Morne Brabant / 35 mins by car on the B9*

It's an enjoyable trip to travel along the coast through the colourful Creole village of Baie du Cap (make sure to snap a photo of the bend in the road here) and on to Bel Ombre. Once in the village, you will be met by beautiful, well-kept beaches, exquisite bars and chic restaurants, and you can play golf, go pedal boating or kite surfing. For a change from the beach life, head to the *Heritage Nature Reserve (daily 8.30am-4.30pm | tel. 6 23 56 15 | heritagenaturereserve.com | ☉ 2 hrs)*, a nature and wildlife reserve laid out

like a small primeval forest. Here you can go on a safari, hiking or quad biking, and see how many animals you can spot from crocodiles to flying foxes and lemurs. There is even a 🐾 petting enclosure with giant tortoises you can feed, and a swimming pool.

Continue on for about 12km on the ⭐ *coastal road to Souillac* which takes you through a landscape of undulating hills, past fishing boats, colourful houses and small Creole shops. Between Bel Ombre and Souillac there is a very special beach, the *Rivière des Galets (⊞ C11)*. You can't swim there, but it's still worth a visit. It's a beautiful pebble beach full of polished black stones, with a fantastic view of the sea and large waves breaking on the shore. The mountain range towers in the back. Your music? The sound of the water rushing over the pebbles. *⊞ B11*

# SOUILLAC

*(⊞ D11)* **The small and seemingly inconspicuous fishing village of Souillac boasts a natural harbour, Hindu temple, church, park, a few shops and a bus station.**

As so often happens, it is its stunning location by the sea that attracts so many holidaymakers.

### SIGHTSEEING

#### GRIS GRIS

Although you are not allowed to swim here, the vantage point at the southern end of the village offers an unforgettable sight. The coast is wild here and the sea thrashes against the rocks; with a bit of luck, you will spy a whale or two through the spray. The car park also hosts snack bars for drinks and a bite to eat.

A little further on and you will come to *La roche qui pleure*, the "crying rock": with every wave that crashes against it, water splashes up the stone and the formation of droplets creates a rainbow of light – stunning!

**INSIDER TIP**
**Beautiful tears**

### MUSÉE ROBERT EDWARD HART 🐷

This site was once the refuge of Mauritian poet Robert Edward Hart, who died here in 1954. Hart was born in Port Louis and was a journalist and librarian before he started to write the poems and novels for which he was honoured by the Académie Française. His house and museum are located right next to the sea on the way to Gris Gris. It displays his furniture, portraits of the poet and copies of his works. *Mon–Fri 9am–4pm, Sat 9am–noon | free admission | ⏱ 1 hr*

### ROCHESTER FALLS

If you ask the boys on the northern outskirts of the village the way to these waterfalls, they'll answer with a mysterious *"très compliqué"* and offer to lead the way by bike – for a price. Indeed there are few signs and it's not easy to find the falls. You should negotiate a price with your guide before starting your drive. Although the water of the Rochester Falls only plummets from a height of 15m, they cover a vast width of rock, which makes this an idyllic spot.

## EATING & DRINKING

### CHEZ ROZY LE GRIS GRIS RESTAURANT

Freshly caught fish, lobster and langoustine. Simple, but really good – authentic fresh dishes of the kind Mauritians cook at home. *Tue–Sun 11am–4pm | Gris Gris | tel. 6 25 41 79 | €–€€*

# AROUND SOUILLAC

### 5 LA VANILLE NATURE PARK 🐾

*7km from Souillac / 10 mins by car on the A9*

This park, near the village *Rivière des Anguilles*, is somewhere you can see crocodiles, monkeys, giant tortoises, small reptiles and bats. Kids can help feed the tortoises *(11am and 1pm)* or watch the crocodiles being fed *(11.30am)*. There is also a farm with chickens, goats and rabbits where visitors can get involved. The beautiful restaurant *Le Crocodile Affamé (€€)* makes its mark with its homemade dishes. *Daily May–Oct 8.30am–5pm, Nov–April 9am–5.30pm | admission 500 rupees, children (3–12) 150 rupees | tel. 6 26 25 03 | lavanille-naturepark.com | ⏱ 1 hr | 🗺 D11*

Most of the work is still done by hand at the Bois Chéri tea plantation

## 6 LA VALLÉE DES COULEURS

*10km from Souillac / 15 mins by car on the B10*

During construction work in 1998, the owner of this park dug fairly deep and discovered that the earth shone in 23 shimmering colours, including grey, blue, red and violet – a geological sensation that turned his fruit and vegetable business into a tourist destination. There's a circular trail with numerous small waterfalls, the pools of which you can swim in. If you're on the hunt for a bit more action, you can whizz across the park on a number of ziplines – from a beginner's version to the extreme option! *Daily 8.30am–5.30pm | admission 400 rupees, zipline from 1150 rupees | northwest of Souillac: from Chemin Grenier go in the direcion of Mont Blanc, then it's signposted | lvdc.mu |* ⏱ *1 hr |* 🗺 *C10*

## 7 BOIS CHÉRI TEA FACTORY

*16km from Souillac / 20 mins by car via the B88*

This tea plantation has a small museum that explains the cultivation, production and refinement of the beverage. A tea tasting session is included in your visit. The *Bois Chéri Restaurant (daily 9am–5pm | booking essential | tel. 54 71 12 16 | €€)* serves excellent food (Mauritian and European cuisine) and there are panoramic views of the ocean and a small lake with swans. The wild deer are known come all the way up to the restaurant's large windows, so you'll really feel you're dining in the midst of nature – while being watched! *Mon-Sat 9am–5pm | admission 525 rupees | Bois Cheri Royal Road | Bois Chéri | saintaubinloisirs.com |* ⏱ *1 hr |* 🗺 *D10*

**INSIDER TIP** *Under observation!*

# THE WEST

## THE MOST STUNNING SUNSETS

Between Le Morne and Port Louis, you'll find a stretch of coast with mile after mile of beach. The climate is mild, and it hardly ever rains. It's holiday heaven, with most of the tourist infrastructure directly on the lagoon and so protected by the coral reef, with views of the turquoise sea and a magnificent mountain backdrop.

It is in the hinterland towns, spread out for miles on end across the plateau and merging into one long urban centre, that a large

Bathing beaches and a rugged mountain backdrop at Flic en Flac

proportion of the Mauritian population lives. There are plenty of shopping centres and markets here, and the range of goods available is more varied than in the tourist centres.

The seaside towns of Flic en Flac, Wolmar and Tamarin have brought an economic boom to what was once a poor region: with beautiful sandy beaches that are perfect for swimming, snorkelling and surfing, it didn't take long for a number of top-quality hotels to spring up. Only the occsaional colonial villa, complete with lush gardens, remains.

# THE WEST

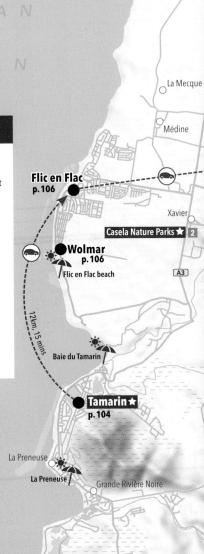

I N D I A N

O C E A N

## MARCO POLO HIGHLIGHTS

★ **TROU AUX CERFS**
Beautiful views deep into the crater of
the extinct volcano in Curepipe and out
across the island ➤ p.102

★ **FLORÉAL SQUARE**
Cashmere and more: shop for high-
quality clothing, perfume and fluffy
rugs at low prices that are partly duty-
free in this mall ➤ p. 103

★ **TAMARIN**
Two rivers flow into the sea at this
picture-perfect lagoon. At weekends,
Mauritians love to barbecue and party
on the beach ➤ p. 104

★ **CASELA NATURE PARKS**
Head out on safari in this wildlife
paradise near Tamarin ➤ p. 105

Albion

La Mecque

Médine

**Flic en Flac**
**p. 106**

Xavier

**Casela Nature Parks** ★ 2

●**Wolmar**
**p. 106**

Flic en Flac beach

A3

12km, 15 mins

**Baie du Tamarin**

**Tamarin** ★
**p. 104**

La Preneuse

**La Preneuse**

Grande Rivière Noire

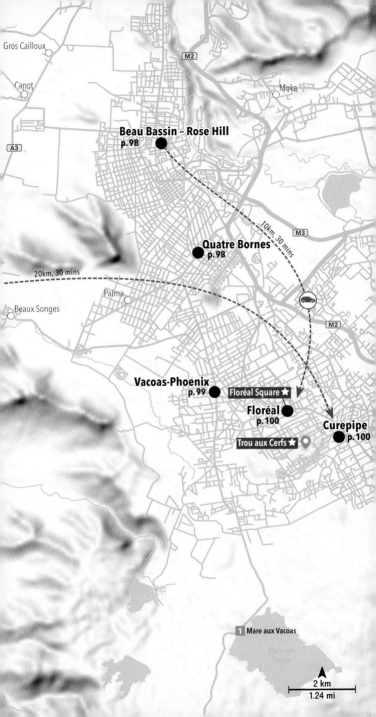

Gros Cailloux

Canot

[M2]

[A3]

Moka

**Beau Bassin – Rose Hill**
p. 98

[M3]

10km, 30 mins

**Quatre Bornes**
p. 98

20km, 30 mins

Palma

Beaux Songes

[M2]

**Vacoas-Phoenix**
p. 99

Floréal Square ★

**Floréal**
p. 100

Trou aux Cerfs ★

**Curepipe**
p. 100

**1** Mare aux Vacoas

Mare aux Vacoas

2 km
1.24 mi

Rose Hill plaza in the rain

# QUATRE BORNES, BEAU BASSIN & ROSE HILL

(∭ C7–8) **Visitors mainly come to Quatre Bornes (pop. 72,000) for the clothes market, where you can buy individual items (knitwear, shirts, jeans, and so on) at particularly good prices.**

*Beau Bassin* is the northernmost of the seven contiguous cities in the western highlands and seamlessly transitions right into *Rose Hill* business city. Life here revolves around the plaza, with its town hall, library and theatre. Just a three-minute walk from the bus station, behind the Sir Gaëtan Duval Stadium, is the *New Arab Town market (daily).* This is where the Mauritians buy their clothing, household goods and food.

## EATING & DRINKING

### LES CAPRICES DE GERVAIS
Exquisite international cuisine and delicious cakes. Also serves breakfast. *Daily 9am–6pm | 128 Route Saint Jean | Quatre Bornes | tel. 4 65 4575 | €€*

### GOOL SQUARE
This unusual snack bar with a red tin roof is somewhat of a cult favourite and provides an exceptional meeting point for night owls. "People who know Gool know they can come late," says owner Bhai Gool, because it's the only place in Mauritius where you can purchase food and drinks around the clock seven days a week – non-alcoholic drinks, of course, as Gool is Hindu. He is from India and something of a philosopher, and he seems to find stimulating conversation more important than selling snacks. *Road at the roundabout by the post office and the police station | Beau Bassin | €*

**INSIDER TIP**
**Open 24/7!**

### KING DRAGON

Excellent Chinese restaurant serving Cantonese food. Very popular with Mauritians. *Tue–Sun | Route St Jean | Quatre Bornes | tel. 4 24 78 88 | €€*

## SHOPPING

Rose Hill's shopping opportunities give Curepipe a run for its money. The most important shopping centres are *Arcade Sunassee* on Royal Road, *Atrium Shopping Centre* on Vandermeersch Street and *Les Galeries Evershine (Mon–Sat 10am–5pm, Sun 10am–noon | Commercial Complex, 5 S Soopramanien Street).* This is where the island's young people like to shop: trainers, clothes, skincare, make-up and jewellery, plus some real gems amid the tourist tat, can be found here. Plus, it's so wonderfully colourful that even if you don't buy anything, you can bask in the inspiration for next time!

*INSIDER TIP* **Get your gear here!**

Designer jewellery is made by goldsmith *Bernd Wilhelm (Draper Av./Belle Rose Av. | tel. 4 67 94 75 | berndwilhelm.com)* in his workshop in Quatre Bornes. Best to make an appointment before you visit.

## NIGHTLIFE

### BACKSTAGE LOUNGE BAR

This bar in the *Hennessy Park Hotel* at the northeastern edge of Quatre Bornes is where Mauritius's rich kids meet for a drink. It's set right in the middle of the futuristic *Cybercity* with its call centres, tech companies, and cool colours and lights. The bar itself even boasts chairs that could be straight out of the star ship *Enterprise*. Every Friday and Saturday evening live music is performed on the terrace. Happy hour is from 5pm to 7pm, with fantastic cocktails and the best rums. *Daily | Cybercity level 65 | Quatre Bornes | short.travel/mau16*

*INSIDER TIP* **Cocktails with style!**

### PARADOX CLUB

This place simply rocks on Fridays and Saturdays. There's a colourful mix of music, or Mauritian musicians perform sega. Always packed. *From 9pm | admission 300 rupees | MCB Building, John Kennedy Street | Rose Hill*

### QUEEN'S NIGHT CLUB

Popular with a mostly younger crowd. Here you can dance into the early hours. *Fri/Sat | admission 300 rupees, some evenings with shows | Route St Jean | Quatre Bornes*

# VACOAS-PHOENIX

*(□ D8)* **It's virtually impossible to define where Vacoas ends and Phoenix begins, so it's referred to by the double-barrelled name of Vacoas-Phoenix. Around 110,000 people live here.**

Many textile factories are located in this urban area, and thousands of people commute to work in the region. It's too urban to spend your holiday here, and it's by no means pretty, but there are interesting shopping opportunities, and Vacoas is easy to reach from Flic en Flac, for example. Every Tuesday and Friday *Vacoas Market (Sivananda Road)* is open in a new market hall.

## EATING, DRINKING & SHOPPING

### CENTRE COMMERCIAL PHOENIX
In this big shopping centre you'll find shoe and fashion stores, a supermarket and a food court. The restaurant *Happy Rajah (daily 11.30am–2pm, 6–9.30pm | tel. 4 27 14 00 | €€)* prepares excellent Indian cuisine. *Mon–Sat 9.30am–8pm, Sun 9.30am–1pm | Sivananda Avenue | centre commercialphoenix.mu*

### THE MAURITIUS GLASS GALLERY
The gallery produces souvenirs from old bottles and jars. Visitors can even witness production and see the secrets of glassblowing for themselves. *Mon–Fri 8am–5pm, Sat 8am–noon | Pont Fer | Facebook: MauritiusGlassGallery*

### OCEAN FACTORY SHOP
This store specialises in leisure- and swimwear and always offers a choice range of goods. *Mon–Sat 9am–6pm, Sun 9am–5.30pm | 56 Nalletamby Road | oceanmauritius.com*

## NIGHTLIFE

### SIRSA
This cinema presents the newest Bollywood films (in Hindi with English subtitles), from romantic love stories to war dramas, and there's nearly always singing and dancing. *Tickets 300 rupees | Royal Road | Castel | tel. 59 11 93 96 | Facebook: Cinema Sirsa*

# CUREPIPE & FLORÉAL

*(□ D8)* **In 1850, when malaria broke out in Port Louis and Mahébourg, whoever could afford to fled to the healthier climate of the highlands. This is how Curepipe was founded.**

With 85,000 inhabitants, it's one of the largest towns on the island and is regarded by many as the unofficial capital, because important public authorities have made it their home. The town also boasts countless stores, good schools and a sophisticated casino. The rich live in the elegant suburb of *Floréal* and some of its colonial villas also house embassies.

## SIGHTSEEING

### BOTANICAL GARDEN 🐷
Although smaller than the large garden at Pamplemousses, this park has just as much charm. **INSIDER TIP** It's home to the *Hyophorbe amaricaulis*, a palm tree that's **An island palm tree** only found in Mauritius. A river runs through the botanical gardens and there is a lake here, too. The lawns are a perfect spot for picnics for those in

need of a break. *Daily 8.30am–5.30pm | free admission | Curepipe | ⏲ 2 hrs*

### DOMAINE DES AUBINEAUX

One of the most beautiful manor houses on the island is on the outskirts of Curepipe. It was built in 1872 and is owned by the Guimbeau family, which also occupied it for most of the 20th century. The décor of the rooms remains almost untouched. You can

city. *Royal Road | Curepipe town limits, in the direction of Phoenix*

### SAINTE-THÉRÈSE CHURCH

A three-aisled Roman Catholic church in neo-Gothic style. It boasts an impressive ceiling with an enormous chandelier as well as stunning mosaics on the floor. *Royal Road | Curepipe*

It has been a very long time since lava spouted from the Trou aux Cerfs crater

take a 30-minute tour followed by a tea tasting session. *Mon–Sat 9am–5pm | admission 400 rupees | Forest Side | tel. 6 76 30 89 | ⏲ 2 hrs*

### SAINTE-HÉLÈNE CHURCH

A church with exceptionally beautiful windows. With a little bit of luck you'll find the stairs to the tower open. Climb to the top for a great view of the

### TOWN HALL

English colonial building dating from 1890, with four corner towers and an open staircase. It's especially beautiful at dusk when it is illuminated. There is also a small park behind the town hall in which you can find Prosper d'Epinay's *Paul et Virginie* bronze statue. *Queen Elizabeth Avenue, opposite St Thérèse church | Curepipe*

Building the island's delicate model ships requires great skill and patience

### TROU AUX CERFS ★

The 650m-high, 85m-deep volcanic crater offers insight into the island's geological history and a view over all of Mauritius. On a good day, you'll even see Réunion, 170km away. The marshy habitat within the crater is surrounded by a woodland grove. The road runs in a wide circle along the crater's edge.

## EATING & DRINKING

### ARCADES CURRIMJEE

Combine relaxed shopping with delicious food in this shopping centre, with five restaurants to choose from. The cosy, retro-style *Bistro Barbu* (Mon–Sat 10am–3pm, Fri/Sat also 6–9pm | tel. 57 46 73 02 | €–€€) has traditional dishes as well as smaller plates, like salads, sandwiches and fish and chips. The burgers are the best – fluffy and spicy! *Chelsea's Cup 'n' Cake* (Mon–Sat 9am–6pm | €) has a menu full of sweets such as fluffy red velvet cake. *256 Royal Road | Curepipe*

**INSIDER TIP**
**From the grill…**

### LA CLÉF DES CHAMPS

You'll find French-Mauritian cuisine and a charming and modern ambience at this popular restaurant. Reservations recommended. *Wed–Fri 11am–3pm, 6–10pm | Queen Mary Avenue | Floréal | tel. 6 86 34 58 | laclefdeschamps.mu | €€–€€€*

### LA POTINIÈRE

This chic restaurant is at the very heart of the Kuanfu-Dubreuil tea plantation in Curepipe. The specialities are seafood and a salad of palm hearts. *Mon–Fri 9am–4pm | Avenue Charles Dickens | tel. 6 70 26 40 | Facebook: La Potiniere Restaurant | €€–€€€*

### LE SAPIN D'OR

Locals simply adore this small restaurant serving simple yet excellent food, including dishes for vegetarians. Choices include chop suey, fried noodles and spicy curry, and the service is attentive. *Daily | Sir John Pope Hennessy Street | Curepipe | tel. 6 98 58 58 | lesapindor.com | €€*

## SHOPPING

For Mauritians, Curepipe is the best town on the island for shopping, boasting *market halls (market days Wed and Sat)*, shopping arcades and factory outlets. The arcades extend along Royal Road. The *Arcades Salaffa (Mon–Wed, Fri/Sat 10am–5.30pm, Thur 10am–2pm, Sun 10am–1pm)* consist of about three dozen shops (mainly boutiques) in the lower or moderate price band. In the *Arcades Currimjee (daily 9.30am–10pm)*, called *Les Arcades for short*, you'll find off-the-peg designer clothing, young fashion, antiques and souvenirs.

### ADAMAS

You can buy duty-free jewellery, watches, and diamonds in this exclusive diamond factory. You can also look at jewellery being made in the workshop. *Mon–Fri 9am–4.15pm, Sat 9am–2pm | Mangalkhan Lane | Floréal | adamasltd.com*

### L'ANTIQUAIRE

Antiques dealer that sells small items of furniture, lamps and dishes – with an affiliated restaurant *(€€)*. *Mon–Sat 10am–5pm | Emile Sauzier Street | Curepipe | tel. 6 98 79 59 | Facebook: AntiquaireMauritius*

### BEAUTÉS DE CHINE

The name gives it away: this shop sells beautiful things from China. Porcelain, carvings, table linen, jade, copper and small antiques. *Fri–Wed 10.30am–5pm, Thu 10am–1pm | Arcades Currimjee | Curepipe*

### FLORÉAL SQUARE ★

Two floors with cheap clothing items like jumpers, polo shirts and t-shirts. Some branded items. *Mon–Fri 9.30am–5.30pm, Sat 9.30am–4pm | entrance in John Kennedy Avenue | Floréal*

### GARDEN VILLAGE

This little mall with shops selling clothing and items for the home, plus a beauty salon, gym and restaurant, is on the way to the Botanical Garden. *Mon–Sat 10am–10pm | Sir Winston Churchill Street | Curepipe | Facebook: Garden Village Curepipe*

### LE PORT SHIP MODEL FACTORY AND SHOWROOM

Admire the handmade *maquettes* in all sorts of sizes in this model ship factory. Buy one on the spot or order a specific model. *Mon–Fri 9am–5pm, Sat 9am–4.30pm | Mangalkhan industrial area | Curepipe | le-port-ship-model-factory-and-showroom.business.site*

## NIGHTLIFE

### CASINO

Apart from roulette, there's blackjack, restaurants, entertainment and dancing to be enjoyed here. You must wear long trousers and sleeves. *Daily 8am–5am | Jerningham Street*

# AROUND CUREPIPE & FLORÉAL

### 1 MARE AUX VACOAS

*7km from Curepipe / 10 mins by car*
The island's largest inland lake, a drinking water reservoir with a hydro-electric power plant, is named after the surrounding *vacoas* (screw pines). Due to its altitude (600m) it's usually cool. With hardwood and pine forest all around, it looks more like Finland than the tropics. *South of Curepipe | ⊞ C–D9*

# TAMARIN

*(⊞ B8)* ★ **Most of the time the town around the wide estuary where the Tamarin and the Rempart rivers meet is very peaceful.**

Between July and September, however, surfers from all over the world flock here to experience the magnificent waves that slip through the gap in Mauritius's coral reef. Inland from Tamarin, the "Matterhorn of Mauritius" dominates: the *Montagne du Rempart* (777m) is one of the landmarks of the island. There are salt flats around this town, which have since given way to settlements – salt ceased to be harvested here a few years ago.

## EATING & DRINKING

### LONDON WAY SUPERMARKET

The London Way supermarket offers an inexpensive lunch, plus coffee and cake. Various Mauritian dishes are nicely displayed behind a glass counter and cost around 250 rupees. Meals can be consumed on the relaxed terrace. *Mon–Thu 8.30am–7pm, Fri/Sat 8.30am–7.45pm, Sun 8.30am–12.30pm | Royal Road*

## SPORT & ACTIVITIES

### SURFING SCHOOL AT VERANDA TAMARIN VERANDA

Cyril Theveneau offers surfboards and lessons from the Veranda Tamarin Hotel. Also open to non-residents. *Daily 9am–5pm | tel. 4 83 31 00 | short.travel/mau23*

## BEACHES

High waves have made the ⋆ *Baie du Tamarin* one of the most popular beaches on the island. It gets busy, especially during the Mauritian winter, between July and September, when there are huge waves; this makes the place a paradise for surfers. Mauritians like to visit the bay at weekends to enjoy family time with a picnic.

### LA PRENEUSE

A quiet, sandy beach interspersed with small pieces of coral. At low tide, a sandbar forms, while at high tide much of the beach disappears under-water. This coastal strip, around 3km long and 12m wide, is located south of Tamarin and many small fishing boats moor here. The evenings bring beautiful sunsets. *B9*

# AROUND TAMARIN

### 2 CASELA NATURE PARKS ★

*10km from Tamarin / 20 mins by car on the A3*

What started as a bird sanctuary is now home to everything from endemic monkeys and sambar deer to zebras, kangaroos and felidae (a type of big cat). Even giraffes, hippopotamuses and rhinoceros have moved in! And of course there are still plenty of bird species to see, including the rare pink pigeon and the Mauritius kestrel. The park is also a paradise for exotic plants and flowers.

Over at Thrill Mountain, you can shimmy across a Nepalese suspension bridge over a 60m-deep gorge, or whizz along a number of ziplines. In the Pangia Kids Park, meanwhile, there is a petting zoo, plus camel rides, miniature golf and some rides for the little ones. If all that is still sounding too leisurely, try zooming down the Tulawaka summer toboggan run.

The *Blue Bird Resto (€€)* boasts panoramic views and is located inside the grounds, as is the *WamWarm Restaurant (€)*, with kids' meals. There are also plenty of snack bars on site.

Montagne du Rempart rises skyward behind the Tamarin river

Daily 9am–5pm | admission from 1,100 rupees, children from 880 rupees, activities extra | Royal Road | Cascavelle | tel. 4 01 65 00 | caselapark. com | ⊞ B8

# FLIC EN FLAC & WOLMAR

(⊞ B8) **The former fishing village of Flic en Flac (pop. 2,000) has managed to retain some of its rural charm, even though it now has the full infrastructure of a holiday resort.**

Flic en Flac is best known for its beautiful beach, although the resort's many widely-scattered multistorey buildings have turned it into a bit of an urban sprawl. Most hotels are located on the southern stretch of beach by Wolmar.

Flic en Flac is only 15km or so south of the capital and offers good bus connections to Quatre Bornes, Curepipe and even Port Louis.

## EATING & DRINKING

### THE BEACH SHACK
Only a road separates this modern restaurant with a terrace from the beach. It serves fresh fish and seafood, salads and sandwiches, plus Chinese soups, steaks and barbecued meats. Daily | Les Sables Complex, Coastal Road | Flic en Flac | tel. 4 53 90 80 | Facebook: The Beach Shack – Mauritius | €€€

## SHOPPING

### CASCAVELLE SHOPPING MALL ☂
This centre with 30 shops, a supermarket and a large food court is located on the left-hand side of the road from Flic en Flac to Quatre Bornes. You can reach it by public transport from Flic en Flac and Le Morne. Mon–Thu 10am–7pm, Fri/Sat until 8pm, Sun until 3pm | cascavelle.mu

### PASADENA VILLAGE
There's a well-stocked supermarket in Pasadena Village, opposite the police station. On the first floor you'll find a tourist information centre and lots of small souvenir and fashion shops. Daily 10am–5.30pm, supermarket open until 8pm | Coastal Road | Flic en Flac

## BEACHES

The 5km-long 🌴 sandy beach at Flic en Flac ranks among the most beautiful on Mauritius. It is an ideal choice for swimming, snorkelling or just strolling. Around 100m from the shore, you can see the waves of the Indian Ocean breaking on the reef. The beach is popular with Mauritians, too, especially on weekends and holidays, when it gets pretty crowded! Extended families bask in the shade of the trees with a picnic. If you didn't pack food, you can find Chinese, Indian, Creole and Italian restaurants for every budget along the coastal road.

Buy an ice-cream before heading to Flic en Flac's popular beach

## WELLNESS

### MARADIVA VILLAS RESORT & SPA

The Ayurveda Spa at this five-star resort hotel offers a wide range of different massages. And the spa professionals have special offers for couples, where both of you can get treatments at the same time, including outdoors. *Coastal Road | Wolmar | tel. 4 03 15 00 | maradiva-villas.de*

### OM SPA

Well-trained staff work in a beautiful space with a calm ambience, decorated in a warm red. Exceptionally clean and quiet. Excellent aromatherapy massages. *Tue–Sun 9.15am–5.30pm | near Pakbo Restaurant, Coastal Road | Flic en Flac | tel. 57 69 26 76 | omspamauritius.com*

## NIGHTLIFE

### KENZI BAR

A yellow Buddha sculpture at the entrance, live music, palm trees, nice people and a cosy Creole ambience will greet you at the entrance. You'll feel like you're sitting with friends in the garden. A popular meeting place. Drinks include cool beer, fruity cocktails and high-quality rums. *Tue–Sun 6pm–midnight | Nenuphar Avenue | Flic en Flac | kenzibar.com*

**INSIDER TIP**
**Relax under starry skies**

# DISCOVERY TOURS

Do you want to get under the skin of the island? Then these discovery tours provide the perfect guide. They include advice on which sights to visit, tips on where to stop for that perfect holiday snap, a choice of the best places to eat and drink, and suggestions for fun activities.

## ❶ "MONDAY'S ROUTE": THE EAST OF THE ISLAND

- ➤ Marvel time and again at the sea view
- ➤ Sample delicious cassava biscuits and buy colourful sari fabric
- ➤ Traipse through the jungle

📍 Mahébourg

 Belle Mare

➡ around 65km

🚗 1 day, 2hrs' total driving time

ℹ Note: it's in the name! Make sure to do the tour on a Monday when the market is open in Mahébourg. Schedule 90 minutes for the walk in Vallée de Ferney.

Get going! The island has much more to offer than hotel pools and beach chairs

## FIRST THINGS FIRST: THE TEMPLE

*Coming from the west on the A 10, as you drive into* ➊ Mahébourg ➤ p. 74, *you will see the Tamil temple* Shri Vinayaour Seedalamen ➤ p. 74 *on your left, and on the right another small temple. Not far away from both there is also a magnificent colonial villa that houses the* National History Museum ➤ p. 74, *which is worth a look.*

## A MAHÉBOURG FEAST

"*Drive towards the bridge that separates Mahébourg from Ville Noire. As you approach the bridge, take the road on the right that passes the Catholic church and leads to the ocean. At the end, turn right then take the first left.* Now you are on the Mahébourg waterfront. *From here, walk via the bus station to the colourful* weekly market ➤ p. 75. Traders sell a range of wares including local fare such as samosas and flatbread filled with vegetables. Polish off your snacks from a spot on the waterfront overlooking the ocean.

*Drive over the bridge and take the second left.* The Biscuiterie H. Rault ➤ p. 75, which produces biscuits from manioc (cassava), is signposted from here. *Follow*

➊ Mahébourg

**11km** 25 mins

the signs to the right, then turn left and right again. *Almost at the end of the road are blue water containers on the left. Turn right there into the bakery's car park.* A tour guide explains the traditional manufacturing methods and afterwards there is the opportunity to sample these delicacies with a cup of tea.

## IMMERSE YOURSELF IN THE RAINFOREST

*Then it's back on the B 28 travelling north from Mahébourg.* The road snakes through a sparsely populated region, going towards the sea, then up into the foothills. Villages are encountered now and then, but the roads are rarely paved. In the nature reserve of ② Vallée de Ferney ➤ p. 77 the authorities are trying to re-establish the original forest. You can get a good impression of the flora and fauna on a 3km walk. From clearings and hills, enjoy the views up to the mountains in the southeast, and of the bay of Grand Port. Hungry now? Ferney Falaise Rouge offers regional fare. *The B 28 will take you further on your journey to* ③ Vieux Grand Port ➤ p. 76. Here you should pay a visit to the listed cemetery and the museum detailing the history of the island's colonisation by the Dutch.

*Now the road follows the coastline.* The Montagne du Lion ➤ p. 77 towers on your left. *Soon afterwards you'll reach* ④ Bois des Amourettes, an idyllic coastal village on this side of the island. From its historic landing stage there is a fabulous view over the ocean to Île au Phare and Île de la Passe in the distance. *A few kilometres further north along the B 28 at Pointe Bambou,* the rustic natural stone house ⑤ La Case du Pêcheur ➤ p. 81 rises out of the water. Have a refreshing drink here before continuing your journey.

INSIDER TIP
**A vast panorama**

**NATURE FIRST, THEN SHOPPING**

*From* Bel Air ➤ p. 81 *leave the B 28 and follow the B 55 westwards towards Camp de Masque.* Along the route, the vegetation starts becoming very lush. From the valley up into the mountain ranges of Montagne Fayence

33km 30 mins

Don't miss Mahébourg's Monday market

and Montagne Blanche, hibiscus plants, banana trees, palms and wild flowers flourish everywhere. *Turn right after Camp de Masque State College by the service station and take the A 7 via Unité to* ⑥ Centre de Flacq ➤ p. 80. Here there are many enticing shops. The small town is known for its Indian clothing stores selling pashminas and metre-long pieces of sari fabric in an array of beautiful colours.

⑥ **Centre de Flacq**

8km 10 mins

**BEACH VIBES**

*Drive along the B 58 until you reach* ⑦ Belle Mare ➤ p. 79. The town's beach is one of the island's most beautiful. There is fresh fruit for sale and, with a bit of luck, people will be dancing to live sega music as the day comes to an end.

⑦ **Belle Mare**

# ❷ SOUTHWEST PASSAGE: A TOUR THROUGH THE CLIMATE ZONES

➤ Barefoot in the magnificent temple of the gods
➤ Steep mountain trek for the fit and determined
➤ Where the earth reveals its true colours

| 📍 | Curepipe | 🏁 | Chamarel |
|---|---|---|---|
| → | approx. 50km | 🚗 | 1 day, including 2-hr drive and 2½-hr hike |
| ▁▃▅ | difficult | ↗ | approx. 800m |
| ℹ️ | Caution, the Black River Peak hiking path (approx. 7km) is covered in scree and often slippery, especially after rain! | | |

**❶ Curepipe**

**9km** 10 mins

**❷ Mare aux Vacoas**

**8km** 10 mins

**❸ Grand Bassin**

## FROM URBAN BUSTLE TO THE LONELY HIGHLANDS

The tour begins in ❶ Curepipe ➤ p. 100. It's one of the rainiest spots on the whole island, with showers every day. But it is worth a visit to see its beautiful churches.

*From* Sainte-Thérèse Church ➤ p. 101 *take the Royal Road southwards and turn right behind Winner's supermarket into Brasserie Road, out of town past the vegetable fields and anthurium plantations. Where the B 64 and B 70 intersect, take the small rural road southwards towards Le Pétrin.* Now you can experience the solitude of the highlands. The landscape is dotted with hills, pine forests stretch into the distance, and mist often hangs above the trees. *Soon you'll reach* ❷ Mare aux Vacoas ➤ p. 104, an enormous reservoir. *On the right is a small car park,* with an uninterrupted view over the water.

## IN THE FOOTSTEPS OF THE GODS

*Back on the road, the route goes uphill. At* Le Pétrin ➤ p. 88, *follow the signpost on the left to the temple complex at* ❸ Grand Bassin ➤ p. 89. The enormous statues of Shiva and Durga in the car park indicate how important the lake is for Hindus. Hundreds of thousands come to its shores for the Maha Shivaratri festival in spring. Otherwise, it is very peaceful here. Semi-tame monkeys leap about and show little respect for the religious offerings. Visit one of the temples, but remove your shoes before entering. The Hindu priest will be happy to explain the various gods to you.

## UP AND UP

*Now return to Le Pétrin on the main road and turn left, heading south. Going via the high plateau of Plaine*

10km 25 mins

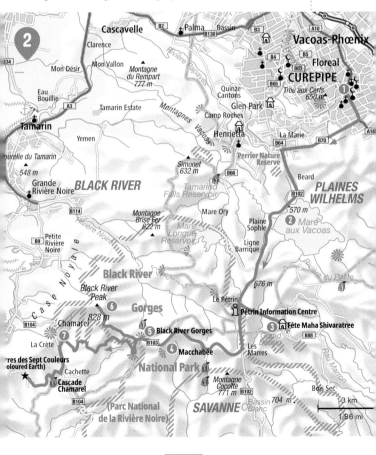

It's a steep climb to the Black River Peak

Champagne (road B 103) you will reach the conservation area of ④ Macchabée ➤ p. 88, the roof of Mauritius, as it were, where the flora is lush. *The road to Chamarel is windy and bumpy; paths branch off now and then into the hidden corners of the highlands.* Signs indicate viewing points. Passing steep cliffs and going through jungle you will arrive at probably the most beautiful viewpoint: the ⑤ Black River Gorges ➤ p. 87. *A path takes you 200m behind the car park,* to a spot overlooking a waterfall. The gorge that the Black River has carved into the mountain continues down to the ocean.

**INSIDER TIP** **Mauritian birdlife!**

The white-tailed tropicbird breeds in the indentations of the rock. You are sure to see one gliding above the river. On a clear day, you may be able to spot the Tamarin plain and the ⑥ Black River Peak ➤ p. 88, the highest mountain on the island.

| | |
|---|---|
| ④ Macchabée | |
| **1km** 6 mins | |
| ⑤ Black River Gorges | |
| **4km** 1hr 20 mins | |
| ⑥ Black River Peak | |
| **10km** 1hr 10 mins | |

*A poorly signposted hiking path to its summit starts a few hundred metres further south on the road, from where you can trek up.* The start of the hike is easy. After about 35 minutes, the view opens up towards the south and on to Le Morne mountain. Then it gets a bit more challenging. The last part is so difficult that you should bring a rope as a climbing aid to help you reach the summit. Once at the top, the magnificent view is more than worth the effort of getting there.

**LET NATURE AMAZE YOU**

After finishing your hike, *continue your journey to* ⑦ Chamarel ➤ p. 86 *and at the entrance to the village make your way to* L'Alchimiste ➤ p. 87 which serves delicious organic food. After lunch, *drive south through the village and follow the signs to Terres des Sept*

⑦ Chamarel

*Couleurs.* The first attraction on the private road through the sugar cane fields is on the left, the Cascade Chamarel ➤ p. 86. *A narrow path takes you up the hill,* where you will be opposite a waterfall on the other side of a gorge – an ideal spot for a photo! Your next destination is Terres des Sept Couleurs ➤ p. 86 *at the end of the road.* Softly undulating sand dunes shimmer spectacularly here in an unbelievable array of colours.

*On the way back, opposite the entrance to a private estate, is the* Curious Corner of Chamarel ➤ p. 86. In this House of Illusions, the laws of nature seem to be forgotten. Feel like a child again and marvel at the sights. Before leaving, grab a snack or ice-cream in the café – you are on holiday, after all!

## ❸ HIKING IN THE BLACK RIVER GORGES NATIONAL PARK

➤ Spot flying foxes and tropical birds
➤ Snack on guavas and pick pink peppers
➤ See magnificent views

| 📍 | West entrance to the National Park | 🏁 | West entrance to the National Park |
|---|---|---|---|
| ⇄ | 9km | 🥾 | 6 hrs, 4 hrs walking time |
| 📶 | easy | ↗ | approx. 550m |

ℹ️ Getting there: arriving from the north, at the entrance to the village of Grand Rivière Noire turn left into a road to reach the western entrance of the park.
The hiking path takes you mainly over scree and goes steeply upwards. Stay on the signposted paths. Away from them, there is a danger of falling down gorges hidden by trees and undergrowth.

**① West entrance**

0.1km 2 mins

**② Visitor centre**

The ① west entrance to Black River Gorges National Park ➤ p. 87 is where it all starts. Information can be obtained from a little ② visitor centre before you begin your ramble under the tall trees into the depths of nature.

### SHOES OFF AND KEEP GOING

The hiking trail is well signposted. *Cross a small bridge and after 500m the path forks. Take the right fork towards the Macchabée Viewpoint. Follow the sign towards the kiosk, and you will soon cross another bridge,* which is often under water, especially during the rainy season. Just take your shoes off as the water is only a few centimetres deep. In heavy rain, the mud runs down in rivulets. It is slippery but the path is not very steep. *After about 30 minutes you'll reach the ③ Kiosk,* a small wooden pavilion. *A bridge crosses the Black River here.* You have to walk ankle-deep in water again. The river winds its way through the tropical forests, where rock faces form one side of the bank.

*After a small bend to the right, you will be hiking upwards,* sometimes over scree, sometimes on concrete

1.4km 20 mins

**③ Kiosk**

1.3km 45 mins

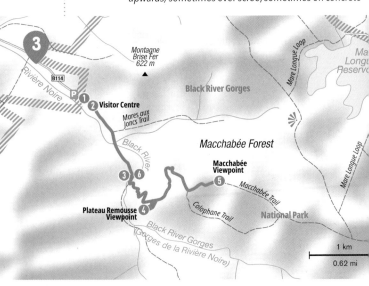

Look out for monkeys in the national park

paths. Admire the views over the lush, green highlands. Tropical birds glide through the gorges and, if you're lucky, you'll see flying foxes leap from tree to tree.

### PICK A RIPE GUAVA

Even further up, the path is lined with guava trees. The fruit ripens in April, so if you're there at that time of year, pick one and try it. Pink peppercorns also grow here and many Mauritians come to harvest them. *After about an hour, the path to the* ❹ Plateau Remousse Viewpoint *is signposted. The flat, grassy path leads to a clearing* from where there is a glorious view over the surrounding mountains and the ocean.

*Back on the main path, continue going uphill. After about an hour and a half – the last few metres are very steep – you'll reach the* ❺ Macchabée Viewpoint. From here you will have a panoramic view of a blaze of colour from forest green to ocean blue.

### COOL OFF

*Take the same way back.* Pause for a refreshing dip in the ❻ Black River. At the ❶ west entrance there is a picnic area with tables and benches. High time to unpack all the tasty snacks you brought with you!

❹ Plateau Remousse Viewpoint

**1.9km** 1 hr 30 mins

❺ Macchabée Viewpoint

**2.8km** 1 hr

❻ Black River

❶ West entrance

# GOOD TO KNOW

## HOLIDAY BASICS

# ARRIVAL

**+ 4 hours time difference**

Mauritius is 4 hours ahead of Greenwich Mean Time, 10 hours ahead of US Eastern Time, and 6 hours behind Australian Eastern Time.

**Adapter Type G**

The voltage is 220/230 volts AC, with three-pin, British-style sockets.

**GETTING THERE**

Air Mauritius *(airmauritius.com)* and British Airways *(britishairways.com)* fly direct to Mauritius from London in 12–13 hours (but not every day). Flights with transfers are offered by Air France, KLM and Emirates, among others. A return flight costs from around £650, and package deals often make your holiday cheaper. There are no direct flights from the United States. Emirates, KLM and British Airways offer flights with transfers from around US$1,500. Flights from New York take around 21 hours. There aren't any direct flights from Canada either, and flights from Toronto often stop in New York or Paris (or both).

Mauritius' international airport is located in Mahébourg. From there, it takes about 75 minutes to Port Louis with bus 198 (cost is around 45 rupees); by taxi it takes about 30 minutes and will cost around 2,360 rupees, the equivalent of around £45, for a trip to the capital.

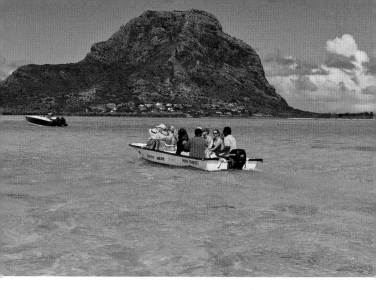

Which beach shall we visit today? Mauritius has so many to choose from!

## ENTRY REQUIREMENTS

British and EU citizens, Americans, Australians, Canadians and New Zealanders need a passport that will be valid for longer than the duration of their stay on the island. Children need their own passport. Anyone travelling from areas affected by cholera or yellow fever must submit proof of vaccination. An entry visa can only be obtained at the airport if you can show that you have a ticket for a flight out and a hotel reservation (or a booking for another form of accommodation).

## VACCINATIONS

Although no vaccinations are required for incoming travellers from Europe, the USA or Canada, you should nevertheless make sure your vaccinations are up to date for polio, diphtheria, mumps, measles, rubella, tetanus and hepatitis A. People travelling from areas infected with yellow fever may need a vaccination certificate. Check with your embassy if you're unsure.

# GETTING AROUND

## BOAT RENTAL

On Mauritius, motorboats can only be rented with a captain; you can't explore the ocean on your own. Small sailing boats and kayaks can be rented in hotels and you're allowed to go it alone within the boundary of the reef.

## BUSES

**INSIDER TIP** The bus experience

If you really want to know what makes Mauritius tick, just take the bus. While it's not necessarily punctual, it willl be cheap, exciting and get you to your destination.

You may find yourself sitting next to a farmer with a squawking chicken in her arms! The bus network is well developed but timetables are not on display, though you can find the schedule on the internet *(mauritiusbuses.com)*. Each town has a central bus station. In urban areas buses operate from 5.30am to 8pm and from 6.30am to 6.30pm in the countryside. Tickets are only available from the conductors.

## DRIVING: CAR & SCOOTER HIRE

Cars can be hired from 2,000 rupees per day (excluding 15 per cent tax and insurance fees). You must be 21 to hire a car. It's advisable to book well in advance in the months of December and January.

You can hire scooters almost everywhere and use them to explore the island. They should not be driven around after dark, however, as locals tend to walk on the roads and can be difficult to spot from a distance. Sometimes dead animals block the roads. You should remain calm when you're caught up in the turmoil of traffic in the towns. Don't just rely on the indicator when you're turning, but stick out your arm too. Better still, get your passenger to do it. If you want to turn left, stick your right arm upwards and lean it slightly to the left-hand side. When turning right, the right arm should be stretched out to the right.

They drive on the left in Mauritius. On roundabouts, the person on the right has the right of way. In villages, the speed limit is 50kmh, otherwise it's 80kmh or 110kmh on the motorway. The motorway between the airport in the south of the island and Grande Baie in the north is of a good standard. The rest of the road network consists mainly of narrow, winding rural roads.

Pay and display parking tickets (valid for 30 minutes each) are available at petrol stations and have to be perforated so that they show the date and time of their purchase.

## TAXIS

Taxis rarely have meters. You need to negotiate the price before the journey and shouldn't pay more than 60 rupees per kilometre. The journey from the airport to Flic en Flac costs around 2,150 rupees (£40). You can also usually hire taxis for the whole day.

# ESSENTIALS

## BEACH SELLERS

Wherever there are tourists, there are beach sellers too. Always assume that the prices are inflated. What are sold as "local craft products" are often cheap imported goods. Have a look in the stores first to get a rough idea of the prices. Then you'll be much better placed to negotiate prices with the beach sellers.

## CRIME

Mauritius is a safe holiday destination. Nevertheless, tourists are recommended to avoid deserted beaches and poorer residential areas, especially after dark, as criminal assaults

# FESTIVALS & EVENTS
## ALL YEAR ROUND

### JANUARY/FEBRUARY
**Thaipoosam Cavadee** (Kalaisson temple, p. 69, and elsewhere). Festival procession, where the Tamil population stick needles through their bodies and carry *cavadees* – colourfully decorated wooden frames.

**Chinese New Year** (Port Louis, p. 66, and elsewhere) Chinese families decorate their house with the lucky colour red, offerings are given in the pagodas.

### FEBRUARY/MARCH (2023-2027)
**Maha Shivaratree** (Grand Bassin, p. 89).
**Holi** Hindu festival of colour symbolising the power of good over evil; people throw powder paint at each other.

### MARCH/APRIL
**Eid-Ul-Fitr** Muslims celebrate the end of the holy month of Ramadan; alms are given to the needy, followed by a feast (no fixed date).

### AUGUST/SEPTEMBER
**Ganesh Chaturthi** Hindu festival in for Ganesh, the elephant-headed god.

### SEPTEMBER
**Père Laval Day** (9 September, Chapelle Sainte Croix, p. 67). Pilgrimage to the tomb of of Père Laval to mark the anniversary of the death of the national saint who selflessly cared for the poor and slaves.

### OCTOBER/NOVEMBER
**Divali** Hindu festival in honour of goddess Lakshmi, who brings luck and wealth to people's homes; houses are lavishly decorated with lights (photo).

### NOVEMBER/DECEMBER
**Porlwi** (Port Louis, p. 67) Culture festival.
**Ganga Asnan** Hindu festival held on the seashore; the holy River Ganges flows into the Indian Ocean, so bathing in the sea gives celebrants purity and new strength
**Teemeedee (fire-walking):** Tamil festival in which celebrants run over glowing coals.

can occur. Be aware of pickpockets, especially in crowded areas like markets. If you change large sums of money, you should take care when leaving the bank or ATM.

## CUSTOMS

Visitors aged 16 and over have a duty-free import allowance of: 200 cigarettes, 50 cigars or 250g of tobacco; one litre of spirits, two litres of wine or beer; 25ml of eau de toilette. Importing weapons, drugs, pornographic material, fruit, vegetables, meat and plants is forbidden.

The export of some shells, especially corals, is prohibited.

### RESPONSIBLE TRAVEL

It doesn't take a lot to be environmentally friendly while travelling. Don't just think about your carbon footprint when you fly to and from your holiday destination, but also about how you can protect nature and culture when you're abroad. As a tourist it is especially important to respect nature, look out for local products, cycle instead of drive, save water and much more. If you would like to find out more about eco-tourism please visit: *ecotourism.org*.

## HEALTH

Mauritius is free of tropical diseases, the island is practically malaria-free, and you don't have to worry about encountering any poisonous animals, either. A high level of sun protection is essential, and using mosquito repellent is advisable. Don't drink the tap water. Because of sea urchins and sharp coral in shallow water, you should wear bathing shoes. Even small wounds should be disinfected right away. Sea urchin stings should be removed by a doctor. Digestive problems can often be helped with a spoonful of black papaya seeds, which are said to have a "stimulating" effect.

There's a ban on importing some medications into Mauritius. You can ask for a list of banned pharmaceutical products in the Mauritian embassy in your home country. The selection of medications carried by pharmacies meets European and American standards. Most hotels work with contracted doctors. Travel health insurance is recommended. Should you need to go to a hospital, you have a choice between government-run facilities, which also treat tourists for free, and private clinics where you have to pay in cash. In the case of severe illness, private clinics are definitely recommended.

## INFORMATION

The website *mauritius.net* provides information ranging from points of interest and a calendar of events to booking opportunities. When choosing accommodation, *mauritius.com* is helpful. The Chamber of Commerce reports in detail at *mcci.org* about every conceivable aspect of life on the island.

## INTERNET ACCESS & WIFI

Most hotels offer their guests an internet connection for an additional fee.

Free WiFi is available at *Cascavelle Shopping Village* in Flic en Flac, *Super U Complex* in Grand Baie, the *Caudan Waterfront* in Port Louis and at the *Ruisseau Creole* shopping centre in Grande Rivière Noire, among other sites. On top of that, there are some internet cafés *(costs 1–2 euros per hour)*, including the *Cyber Arena Internet Café (Route Saint Jean | Orchard Centre | tel. 7 56 04 38)* in Quatre Bornes.

## LANGUAGE

Although Creole is the language that all Mauritians master and speak amongst themselves, English is considered to be the official language. This means that visitors can get by in English when out and about and in hotels. French is also widely spoken.

## MEDIA

There are three television stations that broadcast alternately in French, English and Hindi. Large hotels have their own video channels or satellite TV. English-language newspapers are only available late and in the larger hotels. For the latest news, see the French-language newspapers *lexpress.mu*, *lemauricien.com* and *lematinal.media*.

## MONEY

Rupees (1 Mauritian rupee = 100 cents) can be bought at the airport. Exchange rates in hotels are often unfavourable. There are banks in major towns *(Mon–Fri 9am–3.30pm, Sat 9am–noon)*. Major credit cards are accepted in hotels and larger shops, and can be used to withdraw cash from ATMs.

| HOW MUCH IS IT? | |
|---|---|
| **Coffee** | *£2.60/US$3.50 in a hotel* |
| **Snack** | *£0.25/US$0.35 for 3 samosas* |
| **Wine** | *£5.30/US$7 for a 0.25 litre carafe* |
| **Excursion** | *Approx. £87/ US$108 for a minibus trip with guide and food* |
| **Fuel** | *£1.05/US$1.40 for 1 litre unleaded* |
| **Taxi** | *£10.50/US$14 per hour* |

## OPENING HOURS

Shops open from Monday to Saturday between 9am and 10am and close at different times in the late afternoon depending on the region. In Port Louis closing time is at 5pm; in Curepipe and other cities it's 6pm on workdays. On Thursdays, however, shops close at noon. In Port Louis they also close at noon on Saturdays. In most supermarkets you can shop from 7.30am to 7pm. Markets officially take place from 6am to 6pm but few stalls are open before 8am.

## PHONES

Calls on a foreign mobile network are usually expensive. Voicemail is also expensive: better switch off before you leave home! Better to get a local SIM card for your mobile, available from Emtel or Mauritius Telecom. They are also sold in many of the shops. You can usually dial directly from your hotel phone: one minute's chat costs about £9/US$11.

Dialling codes: for the UK +44 and for the USA and Canada: +1. The dialling code for Mauritius is +230.

## PHOTOGRAPHY
It's prohibited to take pictures at the airport, in ports and around military barracks.

## POST
There are large post offices at the harbour in Port Louis and next to the market in Curepipe, and almost every village also has its own as well. Opening times: *Mon–Fri 8.15am–4pm, Sat 8.15am–11.45am*. Sending a postcard to Europe and the US/Canada costs up to 20 rupees, depending on the size of the card, and a letter costs up to 40 rupees (mailing something to Europe is generally cheaper than mailing to the American continent). Letters usually arrive faster than postcards.

## PUBLIC HOLIDAYS

| | |
|---|---|
| 1 and 2 Jan | New Year |
| 1 Feb | Day of the Liberation of Slaves |
| 12 Mar | Independence Day and Republic Day |
| 1 May | Labour Day |
| 1 Nov | All Saints' Day |
| 2 Nov | Memorial Day for the first Indian immigrants (1835) |
| 25 Dec | Christmas |

## TIPPING
Service charges and 15 per cent taxes are usually already included in the prices listed on menus; however, a tip of up to 10 per cent is normal. Porters usually get 50 rupees per piece of luggage and maids should be given 70 rupees per day. Simply round up the amount when paying taxi drivers.

## TOURIST INFORMATION
### MAURITIUS INFORMATION OFFICE
*Mauritius Tourism Promotion Authority, 32 Elvaston Place, London SW7 5NW, tel. +44 20 7584 3 66, mauritius.net*

### MAURITIUS TOURISM PROMOTION AUTHORITY (MTPA)
*11th Floor, Air Mauritius Centre, President Kennedy Street, Port Louis | tel. 2 03 19 00 | mauritius.net*

## WEIGHTS & MEASURES
Kilometres and miles, and kilogrammes and imperial pounds, are still used in parallel everywhere, although the decimal system was officially introduced in 1994.

## WHAT TO WEAR
You'll need light, casual clothing for Mauritius. You shouldn't wear swimwear to walk around towns or eat in restaurants. From June to September a light sweater may be necessary in the evenings. Umbrellas and raincoats should be taken on every trip to the tropics!

## WHEN TO GO
The peak season is between November and April. Even then, although it's the rainy season, it usually doesn't rain for long. Humidity is around 90 per cent. Temperatures in the day average

around 30°C. The water temperature can reach around 27°C. On the sheltered west coast, the average air temperature is around 3–4°C higher. It's 5°C lower in the central highlands. In the Mauritian winter (May to October), it's just 5°C colder than in summer. You can find out about the weather at *http://metservice.intnet. mu*, and wind and wave conditions for surfers can be found at *windguru.cz*.

# EMERGENCIES

### BRITISH HIGH COMMISSION
*7th Floor, Cascades Building, Edith Cavell Street, Port Louis | tel. 230 202 94 00 | gov.uk/world/organisations/ british-high-commission-port-louis*

### US EMBASSY
*4th Floor, Rogers House, John Kennedy Avenue, PO Box 544, Port Louis | tel. 230 202 40 00 | mu.usembassy.gov*

### CONSULATE OF CANADA
*18 Jules Koenig Street, Port Louis | tel. 230 212 55 00 | canada@intnet.mu*

### CLINICS
*Wellkin Hospital (Moka | tel. 6 05 10 00); Clinique Darné (Rue Georges Gilbert | Floréal | tel. 6 01 23 00); Clinique du Nord (Royal Road | Baie du Tombeau | tel. 2 47 25 32).*

### EMERGENCY NUMBERS
Police: *999*
Ambulance: *114*
Fire service: *995*

## WEATHER ON MAURITIUS

■ High season
■ Low season

| | JAN | FEB | MARCH | APRIL | MAY | JUNE | JULY | AUG | SEPT | OCT | NOV | DEC |
|---|---|---|---|---|---|---|---|---|---|---|---|---|
| Daytime temperature | 31° | 30° | 30° | 29° | 27° | 26° | 25° | 25° | 26° | 27° | 29° | 30° |
| Night-time temperature | 22° | 23° | 22° | 21° | 19° | 18° | 17° | 17° | 17° | 18° | 20° | 21° |
| ☀ Hours of sunshine per day | 8 | 8 | 7 | 7 | 6 | 6 | 6 | 6 | 7 | 7 | 8 | 8 |
| ☂ Rainy days per month | 17 | 16 | 18 | 17 | 14 | 15 | 16 | 16 | 10 | 8 | 9 | 12 |
| ≈ Water temperature in °C | 27 | 27 | 27 | 27 | 25 | 25 | 23 | 22 | 23 | 23 | 24 | 25 |

☀ Hours of sunshine per day    ☂ Rainy days per month    ≈ Water temperature in °C

# WORDS & PHRASES
# IN FRENCH

## SMALL TALK

|  |  |
|---|---|
| yes/no/perhaps | oui/non/peut-être |
| please | s'il vous plaît |
| thank you | merci |
| Good morning!/Good evening!/Goodnight! | Bonjour!/Bonsoir!/Bonne nuit! |
| Hello!/Goodbye! | Salut!/Au revoir! |
| My name is… | Je m'appelle … |
| I am from… | Je suis de … |
| Excuse me! | Pardon! |
| How? | Comment? |
| I (don't) like that. | Ça (ne) me plaît (pas). |
| I would like… | Je voudrais … |
| Do you have… ? | Avez-vous? |

## SYMBOLS

# EATING & DRINKING

| | |
|---|---|
| The menu, please. | La carte, s'il vous plaît. |
| Pleaase may I have… ? | Puis-je avoir … s'il vous plaît? |
| bottle/carafe/glags | bouteille/carafe/verre |
| knife/fork/spoon | couteau/fourchette/cuillère |
| salt/pepper/sugar | sel/poivre/sucre |
| vinegar/oil | vinaigre/huile |
| milk/cream/lemon | lait/crème/citron |
| with/without ice/gas | avec/sans glaçons/gaz |
| vegetarian | végétarien(ne) |
| I would like to pay, please. | Je voudrais payer, s'il vous plaît. |

# MISCELLANEOUS

| | |
|---|---|
| Where is…?/Where are…? | Où est …?/Où sont …? |
| What time is it? | Quelle heure est-il? |
| today/tomorrow/yesterday | aujourd'hui/demain/hier |
| How much is…? | Combien coûte …? |
| Help!/Careful! | Au secours!/Attention! |
| fever/pains | fièvre/douleurs |
| chemist/pharmacy | pharmacie/droguerie |
| open/closed | ouvert/fermé |
| good/ba | bon/mauvais |
| left/right/straight ahead | à gauche/à droite/tout droit |
| broken/garage | panne/garage |
| timetable/ticket | horaire/billet |
| 0/1/2/3/4/5/6/7/8/9/10/100/1000 | zéro/un, une/deux/trois/quatre/cinq/six/sept/huit/neuf/dix/cent/mille |

# HOLIDAY VIBES
## FOR RELAXATION & CHILLING

## FOR BOOKWORMS & FILM BUFFS

### 📖 THE QUARANTINE
A story of family and adventure from Nobel prize winning author JMG Le Clézio (1985). In 1891, two brothers travel to their homeland of Mauritius – for one, it marks the end of a dream, for the other, a journey to find himself.

### 📖 THE LAST BROTHER
Ten-year-old Raj lives on the edge of the sugar cane plantations in dire poverty and suffers at the hands of his father's violence. In her novel (2012), Nathacha Appanah tells the story of how his life begins to change when he meets David, a boy of the same age.

### 📽️ MY FATHER THE HERO
A charming comedy (2003), with a much younger-looking Gérard Depardieu playing a stressed father troubled by his teenage daughter. All this with palm trees and an excellent soundtrack.

### 📖 THE DODO ON MAURITIUS
Photographer and artist Harri Kallio dreamt up a fantasy world where humans never walked the earth and the birds were in power for this coffee-table book (2004) about the extinct dodo.

# PLAYLIST

0:58

**II RACINE TATANE** – KIKALITÈ MO FRÉR
Jamaican reggae meets Mauritian sega. The result? You can't help but get those feet moving.

**▶ BHOJPURI BOYS** – BAIGUN BAGEE
Strong rhythms sung in Bhojpuri, the language spoken by many of those with Indian roots.

**▶ KAYA** – SI MÉ LA LIMIÈR
Political musician who transformed sega, reggae and creole influences into a dynamic new sound.

**▶ CASSIYA** – RÊVE NOU ANCÊTRES
A hit that will get stuck in your head! This popular sega band mixes Indian and Western pop music.

**▶ LINZY BACBOTTE** – L'AMOUR EN ABONDANCE
This charismatic singer is all about celebrating life.

The holiday soundtrack is available at **Spotify** under **MARCO POLO** Mauritius

Or scan the code with the Spotify app

# ONLINE

**MYSWEETMAURITIUS.BLOGSPOT.COM**
This blog belongs to a Frenchwoman who has made Mauritius her home. She posts about shops, restaurants and hotels, with plenty of photos

**BLOG.AIRMAURITIUS.COM**
Air Mauritius is determined to make itself a high-flyer on the web – a blog with great info and fantastic photos

**SHORT.TRAVEL/MAU1**
How to get an Indian motorbike to pass a Mauritian MOT might not be of interest to everyone, but this is the place to go for in-depth answers to any of your island questions – no matter how obscure!

**MAURITIUSARTS.COM**
This online gallery promotes Mauritian art. With its overview of works in galleries across the island, it gives local artists a platform on the web

**DEFIMEDIA.INFO**
All the latest news in French: from politics to the economy and society

# TRAVEL PURSUIT

## THE MARCO POLO HOLIDAY QUIZ

**Do you know what makes Mauritius tick? Here you can test your knowledge of the little secrets and idiosyncrasies of the island and its people. You will find the correct answers below, with further details on pages 18 to 23 of this guide.**

**❶ Why is the Blue Mauritius kept in the dark?**
**a)** It has mildew stains and is no longer fit to be seen
**b)** The mystery boosts its popularity
**c)** Its blue colour would fade if it were exposed to too much light

**❷ Why didn't Paul and Virginie end up together?**
**a)** Virginie fell in love with a sugar baron
**b)** She drowned
**c)** Paul didn't want to commit but Virginie wanted a ring

**❸ Do the trees on the beach sweat and drip?**
**a)** No, don't be silly
**b)** That's what the Creole people tell their children to comfort them when the heat gets too unbearable
**c)** Yes, filaos give off water through their thin needles

**❹ Which are the most widely spoken languages on Mauritius?**
**a)** French, English and Creole
**b)** English, Hindi and Chinese
**c)** French, English and Spanish

Answers: 1c, 2b, 3c, 4a, 5c, 6c, 7b, 8a, 9a, 10a

Trees provide shade on the beach, but is it ever too sunny, even for them?

**❺ How many doors does Villa Eureka have?**
a) 9
b) 19
c) 109

**❻ Who is the island's airport named after?**
a) Karl Auguste Offmann
b) Queen Elizabeth II
c) Sir Seewoosagur Ramgoolam

**❼ What is sega?**
a) A Mauritian national dish with lots of garlic
b) Traditional music for dancing
c) A street name for cannabis

**❽ What is the most common street name on Mauritius?**
a) Route Royale
b) Boulevard du Paradis
c) Rue des Dodos

**❾ What are the tropical storms in the Indian Ocean called?**
a) Cyclones
b) Typhoons
c) Hurricanes

**❿ Was the dodo ever able to fly?**
a) No
b) Yes
c) Only if it wasn't overweight

Main street, Port Louis

# INDEX

## WE WANT TO HEAR FROM YOU!

Did you have a great holiday? Is there something on your mind? Whatever it is, let us know! Whether you want to praise the guide, alert us to errors or give us a personal tip – MARCO POLO would be pleased to hear from you.

Please contact us by email:

**sales@heartwoodpublishing.co.uk**

We do everything we can to provide the very latest information for your trip. Nevertheless, despite all of our authors' thorough research, errors can creep in. MARCO POLO does not accept any liability for this.

### PICTURE CREDITS
**Cover photo:** Île aux Cerfs (huber-images: H. P. Huber)
Photos: huber images: M. Breitung (108/109); huber-images: M. Arduino (46/47, 82/83), A. Comi (6/7, 70/71), R. Gerth (2/3), H. - P. Huber (10), A. Piai (79, 105), Scatè (93), Schmid (19, 102); R. Irek (65); Laif: Heuer (14/15, 32/33), S. Zuder (63); Laif/hemis. fr: W. Bibikow (80), Degas (94/95), J.-P. Degas (front outside flap, front inside flap, 1, 20, 52, 130/131), D. Denger (11), L. Montico (118/119), P. Wysocki (24/25); Laif/Le Figaro Magazine: Prignet (43); Laif/Loop Images: E. Nathan (59); Laif/Redux/NYT: B. Kurzen (35); Look: B. Cannon (101); mauritius images/Alamy: Alberto (98), H. Blossey (8, 12/13), M. Bozhko (back flap), P. Brown (38/39), K. Erskine (132/133), Findlay (9), B. Marty (87), N. McAllister (74, 107), K. Nikitin (114); mauritius images/Alamy/Dbimages (30/31); mauritius images/Alamy/FB-Stock-Photo_1 (50); mauritius images/Alamy/Panther Media GmbH (66); mauritius images/foodcollection (27); mauritius images/Imagebroker (90, G. Fischer (111), M. Moxter (31); mauritius images/lookandprint.com/Alamy: F. Bettex (121); mauritius images/Loop Images: E. Nathan (54/55, 77); mauritius images/Science Source/Biodiversity Heritage Library (22); mauritius images/Westend61: S. Rösch (26/27), mauritius images/Westend61/Fotofeeling (117); mauritius-images/Alamy/Alamy Stock Photos: G. Kurka (44); H. Mielke (49, 88/89); B. Weidt (135); Shutterstock.com/Phuong D. Nguyen (132/133)

### 4th Edition – fully revised and updated 2024
**Worldwide Distribution**: Heartwood Publishing Ltd, Bath, United Kingdom
www.heartwoodpublishing.co.uk

**Authors:** Freddy Langer, Birgit Weidt
**Editor:** Franziska Kahl
**Picture editor:** Gabriele Forst
**Cartography:** © MAIRDUMONT, Ostfildern (pp. 36–37, 110 113, 116, outside cover, pull-out map); ©MAIRDUMONT, Ostfildern, using data from OpenStreetMap, Licence CC-BY-SA 2.0 (pp. 40–41, 56–57, 69, 72–73, 84–85, 96–97).
As a publisher of tourism texts, we present only the de facto status of maps. This may deviate from the situation under international law and is wholly unbiased.
**Cover design and pull-out map cover design:** bilekjaeger_Kreativagentur with Zukunftswerkstatt, Stuttgart
**Page design:** Lucia Rojas

**Heartwood Publishing credits:**
**Translated from the German** by Madeleine Taylor-Laidler, Jonathan Andrews, Lisa Davey and Mo Croasdale
**Editors:** Kate Michell, Rosamund Sales, Sophie Blacksell Jones
**Prepress:** Summerlane Books, Bath
**Printed** in India

MARCO POLO AUTHOR
## BIRGIT WEIDT

The Berlin journalist and author never misses a Sunday picnic on Mauritius. After all, what's not to love: Indian curry, strong rum, rousing sega rhythms, the scent of vanilla, hearty women's laughter and a wide view of the deep blue sea. She fell in love with Creole life in all its vitality and *joie de vivre* and has been travelling on the island for 15 years now.

# DOS & DONT'S

## HOW TO AVOID SLIP-UPS & BLUNDERS

### DON'T SHOW TOO MUCH SKIN
On the street and in restaurants it's considered impolite to go around in overly revealing clothing. In temples, and to an even greater extent in mosques, visitors are expected to wear long trousers and long-sleeved shirts. You should take your shoes off at the entrance.

### DON'T GO NUDE
On public beaches, where local women keep their saris on in the water, people find skimpy swimwear or topless sun-bathing offensive. Nude bathing is forbidden, though topless sunbathing is usually tolerated around the pool in larger hotels.

### DON'T GET RIPPED OFF
Holidaymakers often pay more for a night's stay with half board in a hotel than a Mauritian person earns in a month. This is reason enough for some self-appointed "guides" to set their rates to Western levels. Always fix a price beforehand, and ask about going rates (for taxis, for example) in hotels – this will save you some nasty surprises.

### DON'T EXPECT ROADS TO BE THE SAME AS BACK HOME
Keep your eyes peeled, especially at night, for deep potholes, bicycles without lights, farm workers walking home after a drink and sleeping dogs – it is easy to miss something.

### DON'T CHOOSE THE WRONG SOUVENIRS
Shells and coral belong in the sea and not gathering dust on a shelf! They are prohibited items, even if you are able to buy them locally. Many a souvenir is confiscated by customs officers at the border because of the ban on exports, and they will fine you.